The Liberal Illusion

The Liberal Illusion

DOES TRADE PROMOTE PEACE?

Katherine Barbieri

THE UNIVERSITY OF MICHIGAN PRESS
ANN ARBOR

Copyright © by the University of Michigan 2002
All rights reserved
Published in the United States of America by
The University of Michigan Press
Manufactured in the United States of America
Cav ⊗ Printed on acid-free paper

2005 2004 2003 2002   4 3 2 1

A CIP catalog record for this book is available from the British Library.

Library of Congress Cataloging-in-Publication Data

Barbieri, Katherine, 1965–
The liberal illusion : does trade promote peace?
/ Katherine Barbieri.
p. cm.
ISBN 0-472-11300-3 (acid-free)
1. International trade.   2. International economic relations.
3. Peace.   4. Economic policy.   I. Title.

HF1379 .B363   2003
303.6'6—dc21   2002008286

To my mother,
Antoinette Goldstein,
for her love and support

CONTENTS

FIGURES

TABLES

ACKNOWLEDGMENTS

This book project began nearly a decade ago as research undertaken in my first year of graduate school and continued through my doctoral dissertation. Since that time, the book has changed considerably thanks to the input of countless individuals who have commented on various aspects of my research. Unfortunately, it is difficult to recount all those who have assisted me in some manner, but I wish to acknowledge those who were particularly forthcoming with assistance and encouragement during the course of this project.

First, I would like to thank Stuart Bremer, who as supervisor to my doctoral dissertation aided me in more ways than I could ever recount here. I was fortunate to have had him as a mentor. I cannot thank him enough for all that he has done for me over the years to contribute to my intellectual growth. I am also thankful to him for providing me with the Correlates of War data sets used in this study, for assisting me with assembling the trade data base, and most importantly, for teaching me many of the skills that were necessary to conduct this research. Similarly, the other members of my doctoral dissertation committee were instrumental in the formative stages of this research project. They include Michael McDonald, Glenn Palmer, and Solomon Polachek. Each of them spent countless hours discussing my research and instructing, inspiring, and challenging me.

I was fortunate to have had the assistance of many friends and colleagues who provided feedback on my work. I am particularly grateful to Andrew Enterline and James Lee Ray, who read the numerous drafts of my manuscript over the years and who provided invaluable comments on my research. Their encouragement was critical during many difficult phases of this project. I am also thankful to my friends and colleagues at the University of North Texas, particularly Marilyn Morris and Adrian Lewis, and those at Vanderbilt University, particularly Marie Henehan, Alan Peters, Richard Tucker, and John Vasquez. Many other scholars and friends have provided assistance, comments on my work, and encouragement during this research project. They include Frank and Linda Cohen, Christian Davenport, Nils Petter Gleditsch, Jack Levy,

Zeev Maoz, John Oneal, Brian Pollins, Bruce Russett, Gerald Schneider, J. David Singer, Sue and Doug Young, Talal Zouaoui, the participants of the International Studies Association Workshop on Interdependence and Conflict, and the participants of the Yale Workshop on Interdependence, Democracy, and Conflict. I am also thankful to Oliver Selywyn and Karen Peterson who were valuable research assistants to me during different stages of this project.

Construction of the trade and exchange rate databases used in this research was a long and often frustrating endeavor. Several people provided me with guidance and encouragement. I am particularly grateful to J. D. Singer for providing me access to the bibliographic sources from another trade project undertaken by the Correlates of War Project. Philip Schafer also assisted me in locating trade data and exchange rate sources. Peter Brecke and Brian Pollins provided important suggestions for establishing decision rules for coding the trade data.

Without the love, support, and understanding of my family, I would not have been able to achieve this goal. My mother, Antoinette Goldstein, deserves credit for my achievements, for her love and support provided me with the strength and determination to follow my dreams. My brothers, Anthony and Ernie, have provided encouragement and, most importantly, humor, throughout my endeavor. My father and my extended family have also been a source of support to me during some very difficult times. In addition, Shaka Zulu Barbieri has been a constant source of joy in my life.

Finally, I owe a tremendous debt of gratitude to John Geer. He has stood beside me during much of this project. I have benefited from his insightful comments on drafts of my work, his stimulating discussions, and his love and support during many trying times. I cannot thank him enough for all that he has done for me.

Chapter 1

INTRODUCTION

> The natural effect of commerce is to bring about peace. Two nations
> which trade together, render themselves reciprocally dependent; if
> the one has an interest in buying and the other has an interest in sell-
> ing; and all unions are based upon mutual needs.
>
> —Montesquieu, *The Spirit of the Laws*

> It is really difficult to understand the claim of the free-traders who
> imagine that the more advantageous application of capital will abol-
> ish the antagonism between industrial capitalists and wage workers.
> On the contrary, the only result will be that the antagonism of these
> two classes will stand out still more clearly.
>
> —Karl Marx, "On the Question of Free Trade"

Throughout history policymakers, theorists, and the general public have
debated the virtues and vices of foreign trade. The post–Cold War era
has witnessed a resurgence of these debates, with scholars and policymakers divided over whether trade will produce desirable or adverse consequences within and between nation-states. In recent years, international relations scholars have turned their attention to assessing the
validity of one presumed benefit of trade—the promotion of interstate
peace. Unfortunately, few scholars have investigated systematically the
long-standing liberal proposition that trade promotes peace, nor have
they investigated those advanced by critics of liberalism. A systematic test
of these propositions is critical, since foreign trade has become a central
feature of domestic and foreign policy agendas of many states. Thus,
answering basic questions about trade's impact not only is theoretically
interesting, but also has important policy implications.

Although the Cold War was different than major power hot wars, the
post–Cold War period has been marked by the same type of cosmopoli-
tan rhetoric that followed other major world wars. Liberal scholars and
their policy allies argued that free trade and the expansion of ties between
states was the best way to unite former adversaries, as well as traditional
allies. Liberals employed arguments about the virtues of trade that

included an explanation of how economic interdependence creates incentives for cooperation, reduces misperceptions, and fosters formal and informal mechanisms conducive to resolving conflicts of interest that might arise between states. Moreover, many liberals argued that trade could be and should be used as a substitute for military strategies in foreign policy. This included employing policies of constructive engagement when seeking to alter another state's undesirable behavior, including the target state's internal and external aggression. Here liberals maintain, and many believe, that trade is capable of transforming the most oppressive, authoritarian regimes into peace-loving democratic societies. In fact, some portray trade as the panacea for the earth's scourges, ranging from the distasteful characteristics of human nature to poverty and war.

Unfortunately, the empirical evidence supporting liberal claims linking trade to peace, like other liberal views of commerce, is limited. If policymakers are to continue to advocate trade as a peace-inducing policy, we must first understand whether economic ties are capable of producing the desired effects on interstate relations. In this respect, Blainey's warning about liberal theories of peace, in general, is applicable to the issue of trade:

> Irrespective of whether the creed rests on sound or false premises of human behavior, it still influences international relations. . . . If it is based on false generalizations about the causes of war and the causes of peace its influence in promoting peace is likely to be limited and indeed haphazard. (1973, 29)

I begin my investigation by considering what I refer to as the *unconditional liberal hypothesis*—that trade promotes peace regardless of the nature and context of economic linkages.[1] Then I turn to a discussion of competing propositions advanced by critics of liberalism. My purpose is to underscore the differences that exist in trading relationships and the manner in which these differences might produce outcomes that differ from the liberal model of a commercial peace. Critical theories of economic relationships suggest that trade's impact may vary: some trading relationships may be peaceful, while others are conflictual. In light of these arguments, I outline the conditions under which economic ties should be beneficial and those in which the costs may outweigh the benefits. Doing so will enable me to draw linkages between the presumed consequences that result from different forms of trade dependence and the impact this has on interstate relations. By pursuing such a strategy, I am able to evaluate alternative propositions about the conditions under which trade promotes peace.

For example, liberals claim that the expansion of trade ties should always reduce the likelihood of conflict. In response, critics charge that trade's consequences vary depending upon whether dependence is *symmetrical* or *asymmetrical*. In asymmetrical relationships, the costs and benefits for each actor are unequal, with the more dependent state incurring disproportionate costs and fewer benefits. In such cases, trade relations may create an overall net cost to a dependent state, rather than a net benefit. From critical theories, we see that the motivations that liberals assume deter trading partners from engaging in conflict may not hold. Instead, asymmetrical relations foster potential tensions that are less likely to exist in symmetrical relations. Moreover, even in cases where each state in a trading relationship enjoys absolute gains, critics of the liberal argument contend that real or perceived disparities in relative gains might operate against harmonious interstate relationships. That is, a state may view another state's gains, particularly if greater than one's own, as a loss to oneself. From critical theories we learn that trade does not have a uniform (nor universally pacific) impact on trading relationships. Again, this critical response to the liberal claim has not yet been fully tested.

This study departs from previous research on trade and conflict in several ways. First, I integrate often-overlooked scholarship that advances our understanding of the impact trade has on the incidence and severity of interstate conflict. Theorists often address the relationship between interstate trade and conflict from within a particular theoretical framework, frequently neglecting important criticisms from alternative theoretical positions. By considering a wide range of theoretical propositions, I am able to forge a more complete understanding of the debate. Second, I provide a comprehensive empirical analysis of propositions concerning the trade-conflict relationship. My study includes analyses of the period 1870–1992, based upon a global sample of more than 100,000 observations of pairs of states. By expanding the range of cases beyond previous studies, I am better able to assess the generalizability of hypotheses related to the trade-conflict relationship.

Initially, I examine whether a systematic relationship exists between trade and conflict and whether the evidence supports the claims advanced by liberals or critics of liberal propositions. In order to assess more fully the relationship between trade and conflict, I control for the potentially confounding influence of variables believed to be related to both trade and conflict, such as geographic contiguity, joint democracy, joint alliance agreements, and relative capabilities. These variables have been examined at great length in international relations literature, but they have only begun to receive attention in studies of trade and conflict. In addition, controlling for these factors allows me to consider the separate effects of various forms of interdependencies between states (e.g., economic, political, geographic, and cultural linkages).

Before beginning my investigation of the trade-conflict relationship, it is important to consider the rich tradition that exists on each side of the debate about commerce. For that reason, I begin my story about trade with a step back in time, to understand the key ingredients that guide the debates. I discuss some of the underlying issues reflected in perceptions about commerce. This will give us a better appreciation for the reasons people remain divided in their reading of trade's consequences. Next, I reveal the sources of division over trade that have existed throughout the evolution of free-trade ideology. This might explain why starkly different ideologies about commerce have coexisted throughout history, with people divided as to whether commerce is good or bad, capable of promoting peace or contributing to conflict. I will show that history has revealed an ebb and flow of ideologies supportive of and opposed to free trade. The fact that most eras witness a blend of ideologies about commerce suggests that debates about trade will continue to enjoy a prominent role in world politics.

HISTORICAL ROOTS OF
BELIEFS ABOUT TRADE

Throughout history, scholars and policymakers have debated the virtues and vices of foreign trade (Hirschman [1945] 1980; Irwin 1996; Spiegel 1991; Viner 1937). Advocates of free trade underscore the positive aspects of commerce, including the economic, social, and political benefits of trade, while critics question nearly all of the alleged benefits. Instead, critics tend to focus on the negative consequences of trade and the dependence that arises from it. For those scholars focusing on the beneficial aspects of trade, there is a clear connection between commerce and the promotion of peace or the inhibition of conflict. Conversely, scholars focusing on the negative aspects of economic dependence reject the claim that trade produces the necessary restraints on militarized conflict.

Advocates of foreign commerce and its expansion have been described as free traders, cosmopolitans, internationalists, liberals, commercial liberals, and so on, while critics have been labeled protectionists, isolationists, economic nationalists, mercantilists, or neomercantilists. Regardless of the variations in the labels and the strategies pursued, the sentiments found on each side of debates about trade persist over time. In fact, it is truly amazing to see how little has changed over the centuries in debates about commerce, including the issues and the passions they inspire. This might not be surprising if we consider that the divide over commerce runs much deeper than often portrayed, as it touches upon some of the most fundamental issues that guide alternative perspectives about the world. It may be more beneficial to think about the underlying issues that lead people to such different conclusions about commerce.

The Underlying Issues

If we take a broader historical perspective of the divide between advocates and critics of trade expansion, a number of common themes emerge. These include issues centering on whether it is good or bad to be dependent upon outsiders, whether trade's expansion creates positive or negative changes within and between societies, and whether all actors engaged in or affected by trade benefit from it or care about the unequal costs and benefits accompanying it. In sum, people differ in their conception of whether trade is good or bad for the majority and minority of actors and what impact this and other results will have on actors, societies, and the global community.

Discussions about trade rest on core beliefs about the nature of human beings, their motivations, abilities, and capacity for change. This might sound like a familiar theme in the debate between realists and idealists in international relations, but it is more than that. Trading relationships, pursued through barter or monetary exchange, reflect some of the most basic examples of ways in which humans interact. Therefore, the range of personal beliefs, academic fields, historical precedents, and views about how trade shapes actors and their behavior deserves exploration. While such an investigation is beyond the scope of this book, it is still important to consider why trade may or may not promote peace and why people might differ in their perception of which is the dominant trend in the trade-conflict relationship: peace or conflict.

When we speak of trade we speak of human interaction, and thus the divide as to whether such interaction is good or bad frequently underlies concerns over whether trade is a unifying or divisive force. Jean Bodin (1530–96) "endorse[d] foreign trade not only on economic grounds but also 'to maintain communication and keep up good feeling' among nations" (Spiegel 1991, 91). Modern-day liberals incorporate these views, maintaining that communication and the free flow of ideas are the taproots of interstate peace, while the absence of communication and the restriction of free trade and other interstate interactions are the contributing causes of wars (see Blainey 1973, chap. 2). Trade linkages are assumed to give rise to greater interdependence between nations. Liberals maintain that it is this type of interdependence that forges the integration of communities, that unites people and nations in a common bond. However, trade ties do not guarantee integration; and integration does not guarantee peace. One need only consider examples of various forms of social organizations in which members have much in common to understand that close relationships may either inhibit or exacerbate conflict.

Perceptions about the costs or benefits of trade are frequently tied to beliefs about whether the dependence that arises through extensive linkages fosters peace or conflict. Some believe that interdependence promotes better understanding between actors, the development of shared interests, means through which conflicts of interest may be resolved, and cooperation in general. For others, increased interaction and interdependence may simply heighten preexisting differences and create more sources of animosity.

Within international relations literature, scholars differ about whether contact between states is good for peace (see Nye 1968; Soroos 1977). For some, the greatest hope for peace arises when contacts are minimized (Waltz 1979). According to this view, increased interaction creates more opportunities for conflict. Blainey (1973, 30) provides the most striking commentary with respect to what might be an illusory hope for peace through interstate bonds in his reminder that "the frequency of civil wars shatters the simple idea that people who have much in common will remain at peace." In fact, civil wars are as common as interstate wars (see

Small and Singer 1982, chaps. 12–17). Those who argue that peace is the natural result of integration ignore the wide range of behaviors present in close relationships.

Forbes (1997), in his recent book *Commerce, Conflict, and the Contact Hypothesis,* explains that beliefs about the impact of increased contact are similar whether we are speaking about individuals, racial or ethnic groups, communities, or nation-states. Supporters of racial integration in the South, for example, viewed expanding economic dependence and the increased interactions that accompany such dependence to be a means to unify groups and eradicate animosities. The same arguments have been used to support integration between other types of groups ranging from belligerents in religious conflicts to nation-states. In each case, supporters believe that increased contact and mutual dependence will eradicate differences and unify actors in peaceful bonds, while critics have a dimmer view. Thus, we have the free traders on one side portraying a more peaceful and prosperous world arising from the creation of a global economy unimpeded by national rivalries. On the other hand, economic nationalists and realists warn of the dangers associated with increased dependence upon outsiders and the conflicts that might ensue.

People seem to want an answer to the question of whether interdependence is good for peace, but the answer may not be that simple. Interdependent actors may be more likely to exhibit conflictual *and* cooperative interactions (Azar and Eckhart 1978; Coser 1956; de Vries 1990; Sayrs 1990; Simmel 1955; Soroos 1977). De Vries (1990, 431–39) argues that "interdependence is . . . a catalyst increasing the intensity level of international relations in both conflictual and cooperative situations. . . . Interdependence goes along with serious disputes and intimate cooperation, and independence with indifference." Coser argues that "conflict is more passionate and more radical when it arises out of close relationships. The coexistence of union and opposition makes for the peculiar sharpness of the conflict" (1956, 432). When one considers the intensity of conflict found within families, communities, and nations, it becomes clear that the most intense forms of violence are usually found among actors that have a high frequency of interactions and who are intimately connected. Rather than accepting without question the claim that increased contact is good for peace, we must assess empirically whether the interdependence that arises through commerce does, in fact, promote peace.

Coexisting Ideologies

While the view that trade promotes peace is most commonly associated with liberalism, this belief, like those expressed by critics, can be found in ancient writings. Jacob Viner recounts the long tradition of optimism associated with trade:

> In the ancient Greek and Roman classics is to be found the doctrine that differences in natural conditions in different countries made trade between these countries mutually profitable. The early Christian philosophers took over this doctrine and gave it a theological flavor. God had endowed different regions with limited but varied products in order to give mankind an incentive to trade, so that through a world economy they would become united in a world society, and as children of one God they would learn to love each other. This was apparently common doctrine among the English theological writers of the sixteenth century and later. (1937, 100)

Yet, many ancient writers were skeptical about exposing their communities to the influence of foreigners and were distrustful of traders (Irwin 1996; Neff 1990; Spiegel 1991). Aristotle and Plato were among the first philosophers noted for stressing the importance of economic self-sufficiency, warning about the dangers of foreign dependence, and pointing out the corrupting moral influence that could be fostered by way of exposure to foreigners and trade. Greek and Roman philosophers were not alone in expressing their concerns about commerce; Neff identifies similar arguments in ancient Chinese and Indian writings (1990, 11–14). Positive images of traders began to emerge in the Middle Ages, but these views still competed with the more prevalent negative view of foreign trade and the moral fiber of those who engaged in it.

The overriding concern of critics of trade generally centers first on the concern that any infringement upon one's autonomy creates vulnerabilities that could be exploited at a later date. This concern existed in ancient times and still exists today. Descriptions of the liabilities of dependence in international relations resemble those of the dangers of becoming too dependent upon another person. Dependence creates opportunities for manipulation; it gives the less dependent actor an opportunity to exert influence.

As attitudes about commerce evolved through the ages, protectionists have altered some of the strategies they promote for achieving their goals, but their underlying concerns about maximizing self-sufficiency and minimizing dependence persist. For example, during ancient times when issues of scarcity in food supplies were a chief concern to people, leaders regulated and often prohibited exports. Exporters could be viewed as traitors, denying their fellow country-people scarce food supplies for the sake of profit. Imports, on the other hand, were encouraged, since they reduced food shortages, and importers were viewed more favorably for being willing to take risks to feed their neighbors (Neff 1990). Later, mercantilists had a different view of exports and imports, advocating policies that encouraged exports and discouraged imports. The concern here was that owing foreign countries more than one earned sent precious metals outside one's country and depleted resources needed for security. Draining one's war chest seemed to be of greater concern than the risk entailed by curtailing food imports. Ironically, restrictions on food imports generated their own threat to security during times of scarcity, when, for example, Britain retained its Corn Laws in the face of widespread hunger and starvation. Today, political rhetoric favoring exports over imports points to the strong legacy of mercantilist sentiment that remains under the surface even in periods characterized by support for free trade. In fact, one could argue that the tendency for industrial states to protect their agricultural sector could be traced to the underlying fears that survival, at a minimum, requires that a state be able to feed its own people. Beliefs about the benefits of focusing on one's comparative advantage seem to go out the window when faced with the notion of relying on outsiders for the most basic security need—food.

We see that, even today, protectionists continue to view trade dependence as a means through which foreigners could exert undue influence. Critics of open commerce continue to focus on the negative impacts for dependent states that result from the power accorded to the less dependent state in an economic relationship. Free traders agree that interdependence limits state sovereignty, but they believe the benefits afforded through economic openness far outweigh the consequences of limited autonomy.

In the eighteenth and nineteenth centuries, French Physiocrats and classical political economists provided the clearest articulation of a system of free trade that they believed would lead to international peace and prosperity. Proponents of free trade challenged mercantilist views that pitted states against each other in a competitive system of international relations, instead arguing that impediments to trade should be broken down so that all states might benefit from economic freedom. For classical liberals, trade was seen as a force for economic growth and political progress, and as a positive moral force for harnessing the more distasteful characteristics of human nature, such as greed, and channeling them into productive ventures (Hirschman 1977, 1982; Spiegel 1991). John Stuart Mill (1848a), in his *Principles of Political Economy*, maintained that "commerce" was "rapidly rendering war obsolete, by strengthening and multiplying the personal interests which are in natural opposition to it" (quoted in Hirschman [1945] 1980, 10). The classical liberals opposed any state actions that would impede the free flow of trade. Trade restrictions by any state, these theorists argued, could harm more than the intended target of economic barriers and thus be deleterious to the international political economy. Neff (1990) notes, however, that the views of the classical political economists in advocating the creation of a global economic community coexisted with the creation of an international legal doctrine that gave primacy to the state in economic and other matters. The principle of state sovereignty enshrined in international law afforded economic nationalists the ability to assert their parochial interests over those of the global community. The tensions over state versus global interests are relevant to contemporary debates about whether cooperation among self-interested states can emerge through trade and whether supranational interests forged through interdependence can replace national interests. Can the bonds created through economic ties offer sufficient restraints to prevent states from pursuing national objectives that may ultimately lead to conflict?

Today, most people overlook the fact that classical liberals spent a considerable amount of time addressing the negative consequences of the rapid expansion of commerce and capitalism. Adam Smith himself warned about the dangers of the unfettered expansion of capitalism as he watched the Industrial Revolution, and the economic hardships it created for some, take hold. The sentiments of some classical liberals appear to foreshadow the work of Karl Marx, who provided the most thorough critique of classical liberal ideals. The growing pains associated with rapid industrialization, often viewed as intricately linked to the expansion of capitalism and free trade, provide a useful reminder that the consequences of trade are not all beneficial. The question, of course, is the downside of trade and how extensive it might be. Contemporary liberals seem less cognizant of the negative impact of trade than were their nineteenth-century counterparts.

Although notions of free trade, capitalism, industrialization, and development are intricately linked, the issue of trade and its impact on conflict is my principal concern here. The trade-promotes-peace hypothesis is not contingent upon the type of economic or political system a state possesses, one's level of development, or industrial capacity. All these factors may affect trade, but they should not affect the trade-conflict calculus. For commerce is said to overcome the differences that divide communist and capitalist, industrialist and agriculturist, and to unite friends and foes.

As we look to the future in considering the current climate in which free-trade ideology appears to be the dominant sentiment, we must remember that the international landscape seems to witness the ebb and flow of positive and negative sentiments about trade. Periods of global economic expansion, in which philosophies of free trade have flourished, have been followed by retrenchments to ideas of economic nationalism and trade restrictions (see Neff 1990). Generally, a blend of economic philosophies and national policies has coexisted and continues to coexist in the international arena. Even the post–World War II system, which many portray as a period of unprecedented advances in global integration, witnessed corresponding efforts of states to retain control over their economic policies and to pursue national objectives that contradicted the notion of promoting the good of the world community/economy.

In sum, the motivations for trade restrictions can be traced to the basic skepticism about trade's consequences and a desire to control trade in order to limit its adverse effects, while also maximizing its potential benefits. The efforts of individual states to manipulate trade policies testify to the skepticism that trade will produce universal benefits. Yet, net benefits and mutual benefits are very different things. Liberals have never claimed that benefits would be distributed equally among participants in trade. They have, however, argued that all states and the global community, as a whole, would be better off economically and politically in a world free of trade restrictions.

Given the differing arguments regarding trade's consequences for nations, it is easy to see why theorists disagree about the potential impact of trade ties on international relations. If one accepts the liberal portrayal of trade's benefits, one might understand why states would wish to alter their behavior to preserve trade ties. However, for those who question the assumption that trade provides more benefits than costs it is difficult to draw the connection between trade and peace. In general, much of the trade-conflict debate centers on the question of whether the benefits of trade outweigh the costly aspects of economic interdependence. The cost-benefit calculus may differ depending upon the type of trading relationship that exists.

FROM TRADE TO INTERDEPENDENCE

Scholars on all sides of the trade-conflict debate tend to use the terms *trade, interdependence,* and *mutual dependence* almost interchangeably. However, these terms may mean very different things to different people. The term *interdependence,* in particular, has been used to describe myriad relationships in world politics and has been applied to people, nations, and the global community as a whole. I am concerned specifically with the interdependence that arises through trading relationships. I assume that the expansion of trade ties will lead to other forms of interdependence—economic and noneconomic. But I am not specifically exploring those types of bonds, other than to control for them in my empirical analyses. At the same time, my distinction between trade and other forms of interstate bonds is made only loosely, since the important theoretical distinction I make in this study is not between the types of interdependence that exist between states, but between interdependence and the other types of relationships that could emerge through trade. Namely, I explore the theoretical and empirical distinctions between interdependence, dependence, and relative independence. Of course, such relationships are not mutually exclusive and are better viewed in terms of degree, rather than kind.

Throughout the study the term *interdependence* is used to describe relationships of extensive and important interstate linkages, similar to those represented by various forms of alliances. The ties must be extensive to constitute interdependent, as opposed to relatively independent, relationships. And trading partners must be mutually dependent to constitute interdependent, as opposed to dependent, relations. As Keohane and Nye explain:

> In common parlance, *dependence* means a state of being determined or significantly affected by external forces. *Interdependence,* most sim-

ply defined, means *mutual* dependence. Interdependence in world politics refers to situations characterized by reciprocal effects among countries or among actors in different countries. . . . Where there are reciprocal (although not necessarily symmetrical) costly effects of transactions, there is interdependence. Where interactions do not have significant costly effects, there is simply interconnectedness. (1977, 8–9, emphasis in original)

Thus, two distinctions are made—one between dependence and interdependence, the other between interdependence and interconnectedness. For some theorists the mere existence of trade ties between states constitutes mutual dependence.[2] Other scholars distinguish transactional flows between states, or what Keohane and Nye (1977, 9) refer to as interconnectedness, from relations of interdependence. Interdependence entails a vulnerability and sensitivity not found in less extensive linkages.[3] I assume that interconnectedness only gives rise to interdependence when the bonds between states become extensive and salient. Similarly, I assume that dependence gives rise to interdependence only when mutual need exists.

Many scholars agree that highly unequal dependence produces a dynamic very different from the dependence existing in relations of mutual need (see chap. 2). Liberals tend to neglect this analytical distinction when describing the benefits of trade, but neo-Marxist theorists have highlighted the contrast between types of dependence. Dependency theorists, in particular, explain how asymmetrical dependence affords the more independent state a position of power over the dependent state, such that the latter becomes vulnerable to political and economic manipulation. In addition, for radical economists, the costs and benefits of trade are assumed to be highly unequal in relations of dependence. Dependency theorists often draw upon Dos Santos's definition of dependence:

By dependence we mean a situation in which the economy of certain countries is conditioned by the development and expansion of another economy to which the former is subjected. The relation of interdependence between two or more economies, and between these and world trade, assumes the form of dependence when some countries (the dominant ones) can expand and can be self-sustaining, while other countries (the dependent ones) can do this only as a reflection of that expansion, which can have either a positive or a negative effect on their immediate development. (1970, 231)

In this study, I consider the distinction between trade dependence and interdependence. Although these relationships are often viewed in dichotomous terms, I argue that it is more useful to view them on a continuum ranging from relative independence to asymmetrical dependence to interdependence, where characteristics associated with each phenomenon may coexist.[4]

STUDY OUTLINE

The next chapter sketches the theoretical propositions concerning the relationship between trade and conflict that cut across paradigmatic approaches. I review relevant theoretical and empirical work, divided into three broad treatments of the trade-conflict relationship: (1) the interdependence theorists and liberal economists, who posit a negative relationship between trade and conflict; (2) dependency theorists and others who argue that the effect of economic ties on interstate relations is contingent upon whether dependence is symmetrical or asymmetrical; and (3) those who argue that expanded trade ties increase conflict. In addition, a possibility of a fourth scenario is discussed—that trade has no significant effect on interstate conflict. I propose a strategy to evaluate these alternative arguments about trade and conflict.

In chapter 3, I derive a set of testable hypotheses based on these various arguments and establish criteria for evaluating whether the evidence provides support for the unconditional liberal hypothesis or alternative hypotheses. I then discuss a strategy for capturing variations in different theoretical conceptions of dependence, interdependence, and conflict. In addition, I review various methodological problems associated with the data and discuss approaches to addressing potential biases created from the data. Chapter 3 also investigates the evidence supporting divergent theoretical propositions about the relationship between interdependence and conflict.

Chapter 4 moves beyond the initiation stage of conflict to investigate whether interdependence affects the characteristics of conflicts that arise between states. In particular, I examine whether the intensity of conflict occurring among interdependent dyads is greater than that found in less involved relations. Deficiencies encountered in focusing exclusively on economic interpretations of the trade-conflict relationship are raised and discussed. Drawing on psychological and sociological theories of intimate relations, I consider whether the dynamics of close relations differ from those found in other types of relationships. The chapter examines empirically whether interdependent dyads are better able to resolve conflicts through negotiation and whether this prevents dyads from escalating their disputes to the most severe forms of conflict, including wars.

Chapter 5 examines the extent to which the trade-promotes-peace proposition obtains at alternative levels of analysis. I evaluate propositions cast at the national and system levels of analysis and provide evidence that trade's impact on conflict might vary, depending upon where we focus our analysis. In the final chapter, I summarize the findings and discuss their implications for policymakers. I also consider the relevance of the findings for related academic debates and outline an agenda for future research.

Chapter 2

THEORIES OF THE TRADE-
CONFLICT RELATIONSHIP

Before turning to specific propositions about the trade-conflict relationship, I assess the central differences in the theoretical debates that drive
the study of international relations. The theoretical perspective one
embraces may affect his or her approach to analyzing the trade-conflict
relationship. Of course, this fact is not peculiar to this field; scholars recognize that personal biases frequently affect one's research. However,
many people accept standard economic assumptions about international
trade as theoretically neutral and often treat economic theories as if they
were laws. Similarly, people frequently assume that social-scientific
inquiry presupposes the objectivity of the researcher. We must therefore
remind ourselves about the ways in which a scholar's theoretical perspective influences his or her research.

My goal here is to develop a means to integrate alternative theoretical
perspectives and recognize their complementary nature. Furthermore,
many theoretical perspectives that do not directly address the trade-
conflict relationship per se may inform our understanding about the
costs and benefits of trade, enabling us to infer the logical consequences
of some additional debates about trade's impact on domestic or international conditions that are relevant to the trade-conflict debate. For example, the theoretical notions about the consequences of trade on domestic
conditions are relevant to liberal assumptions about the impact of trade
on international relations. Thus, this chapter draws linkages between
those theories that address the domestic consequences of trade and those
that focus directly on the impact of trade ties on interstate relations.

When juxtaposed, the three dominant perspectives in international
relations—liberalism, realism, and Marxism—provide a clearer picture
of the trade-conflict relationship than can be obtained by considering
any one in isolation. The tendency to approach issues of trade and other
economic relationships from a single ideological position often leads
scholars to neglect the valuable insights advanced by alternative schools
of thought. Inevitably, this tactic hinders our ability to advance our
understanding of the relationship between trade and interstate conflict.

Although I make an effort to distinguish the central differences between several schools of thought, a strict and useful typology of theoretical approaches is difficult, if not impossible, to construct. As with any theoretical categorization, particularly one examining several academic disciplines, it is difficult to reconcile inconsistencies that exist within one theoretical tradition in addressing a particular question (e.g., there is no unified voice among the challenges to liberalism). For this reason, it is useful to consider a number of propositions that emerge across, rather than within, particular schools of thought. After briefly discussing major differences in worldviews, I organize my discussion about the trade-conflict relationship according to the predictions that various theorists might make about it. These basic divisions in worldviews suggest why scholars may diverge in their evaluation of trade's consequences and its possibilities for promoting peace.

DIFFERENCES OF PERSPECTIVE

A critical distinction noted about the dominant perspectives in international relations centers on the identification of the *primary actors* in world politics and the appropriate level of analysis on which to focus one's inquiry. Liberals tend to focus on the individual and the state; for the realist, the state is the most important actor in international relations; and for the Marxist, economic class is the key unit of analysis. Propositions emerging from these three schools about trading relationships have been framed in a manner that makes them appear applicable to all actors and levels of analysis. Yet, where analysts choose to focus their inquiry may have important implications for the conclusions reached. It is important to remain cognizant of the fact that trade's impact might vary at the individual, class, state, and global levels, while also recognizing that attention to each level informs our overall understanding about the phenomenon of interdependence. Scholars often overlook the distinction between alternative foci (Singer 1961).

For example, classical liberals spoke about the benefits of trade for individuals and saw these same benefits as applicable to nations. Others may talk about the process of globalization or systemic interdependence and discuss the negative consequences for states and subnational actors. Moving down the scale of aggregation (from system to individual) often highlights the variations that exist within the system or state. In this study, I focus on the impact of trade on relations between states, but many of the theories relevant to the discussion are cast at different levels of analysis. Further exploration is needed to uncover the ways in which trade's impact varies across levels of analysis: different initial definitions of the central actors in international relations may lead to significantly different conclusions.

Another issue of contention among different theorists may be found in the notion of the national interest, which has important implications for the topic at hand. Liberals view state action as driven by a desire to maximize social welfare. Trade is seen as a vehicle to achieving this goal. In this sense they differ from realists, who see states as motivated by power maximization. With respect to trade, realists reiterate mercantilist philosophies, viewing economic statecraft, including trade policies, as one of many instruments available to states in their pursuit of power. Marxists also recognize the desire of states to maximize wealth, but believe this goal is pursued to benefit particular classes, rather than society as a whole. For Marxists, the state is not a unitary actor, but is a structure representing the interests of the dominant classes in society. Neo-Marxists maintain that the state is fundamentally an instrument of class domination. The Marxist rejection of the liberal and realist assumption of the neutrality of the state vis-à-vis class interests leads to the conclusion that trade policies do not benefit all individuals within society, but in fact promote the interests of the dominant classes.

Alternative perspectives concerning the motivations driving state action have important implications for arguments about whether trade ties have the capacity to foster peace among states. If one accepts the liberal assumption that states' ultimate goal is the promotion of national welfare, then it is conceivable that trade and peace promote these goals.[1] If, on the other hand, one accepts the realist view that all foreign policy, including trade, exists for the purpose of achieving national security or power, then trade relationships may be viewed as temporary arrangements that can be easily broken when conditions necessitate other strategies to secure national interests. Realists do not rule out the utility of force—even against a trade partner—when the national interest is at stake. However, force may be undesirable when the trading partner is vital to the national interest. Finally, Marx himself recognized the conflict endemic in economic relations, which suggests that violence may be an integral component of such relations ([1887] 1906). This contrasts with the liberal view that economic relationships deter or serve as a substitute for violence.

I assume states pursue policies designed to maximize both power and plenty. At times a state must subordinate short-term wealth in the hopes of greater power in the long term or may sacrifice power in the short term for the sake of long-term wealth. In fact, limiting one's autonomy through economic ties in the hopes of deriving greater economic benefits would be one example of the latter, whereby the state assumes it can use that wealth for power-augmenting ventures. On the other hand, a state might direct investments into military resources, postponing other productive ventures for the sake of long-term objectives. In sum, wealth and power are complementary goals. For example, states may pursue economic policies that reduce national autonomy in the short term for the sake of acquiring additional wealth to secure power in the long term, or states may incur short-term economic losses to contribute to long-term security goals. This notwithstanding, different perceptions of the national interest may influence scholars and policymakers concerned with trade and conflict.

In a similar vein, a scholar or policymaker's view of *human nature* and of the possibilities or limitations to cooperation and peace in an anarchic world have dramatic effects on the way theorists view the potential impact of trade relations (Stein 1990, 4–13). Classical liberals devoted a considerable amount of energy toward addressing the means by which one could harness human vices. The drive for material gain was considered one of many instinctual vices, but classical liberals viewed it as less dangerous than the others, such as the acquisition of power and glory or seeking revenge (Hirschman 1977). Within the liberal tradition, competition and self-interested action promote the common good. The classical liberal economic system is not built upon the belief that individuals are directly concerned with the public good. Instead, the public good is a positive externality that arises from individual pursuit of self-interested objectives. Adam Smith argues:

> He intends only his own gain, and he is in this, as in many other cases led by an invisible hand to promote an end which was no part of his intention. Nor is it always the worse for the society that it was no part of it, by pursuing his own interest he frequently promotes that of the society more effectually than when he really intends to promote it. ([1776] 1937)

The liberal view that self-interested action can produce desirable outcomes is seen in various permutations of the liberal tradition and continues within international relations theories of cooperation (e.g., Axelrod 1984). For liberals, even if trade policies are motivated by self-interest, they lead to cooperative strategies and peaceful relations among actors. Realists are less optimistic about human nature; they envisage conflict (rather than cooperation or the common good) to result from self-interested action. Each state's pursuit of its own national interest—power maximization and security—produces a security dilemma, which in turn results in greater insecurity and intensifies threats to interstate peace. Although interstate cooperation may emerge, cooperative arrangements are transitory—today's ally may be tomorrow's adversary. Marxists subscribe to a conception of human nature that is similarly skeptical. For Marxists, conflict permeates social relations between classes and between factions of capital (Marx [1887] 1906). The Marxist assessment of human nature offers a glimmer of hope that the demise of capitalism will produce a positive transformation in social relations; yet, until that point, conflict remains ever present. The realist and Marxist positions stand in sharp contrast to the liberal scenario of a common good resulting from egoistic action, which in turn has implications for the ways in which theorists from these schools of thought view trading relationships.

Finally, we must consider the normative concerns of scholars. Liberals pursue different theoretical priorities than do realists and Marxists. Although concerned with issues of peace and war, liberal inquiries focus primarily on welfare issues. Realists are concerned with issues of national security, and Marxists focus on issues of poverty and equity within and between states. This leads to obvious differences in the normative priorities for evaluating trade's consequences. For example, trade may lead to greater welfare, if we think of welfare as an increase in national income, while at the same time insecurity and inequality within and between nations might grow. Again, where scholars focus their attention may lead to alternative conclusions about trade's costs or benefits.

Recognizing the differences that exist across worldviews might lead one to conclude that theorists often look at different worlds and do so with different evaluative techniques. Yet, it is possible to tease out propositions that may be interwoven to capture a more enhanced understanding of the potential relationship between trade and conflict. For example, if I assume that welfare, security, and equality are each important normative concerns, I can adopt a more holistic approach for evaluating the conditions under which trade might contribute to peace or conflict.

THREE HYPOTHESES ABOUT TRADE AND CONFLICT

As noted in the previous chapter, three propositions about the trade-conflict relationship are easily identified in the relevant literature: (1) the liberal proposition asserting that trade promotes peace; (2) the proposition, advanced by neo-Marxists, that symmetrical economic ties may promote peace, while asymmetrical relations stimulate conflict; and (3) the proposition that trade increases conflict. Of course, we need to consider a fourth possibility—the null hypothesis, that there is no relationship between trade and conflict. I will discuss each proposition in turn.

The Liberal Claim: Trade Promotes Peace

The linkage of trade to peace and prosperity enjoys a long tradition in both economics and political science.[2] The trade-promotes-peace proposition can be traced to ancient writings, but it is most commonly associated with the liberal school of thought (Angell [1911] 1972; Blainey 1973, chap. 2; de Wilde 1991; Doyle 1997, chap. 7; Selfridge 1918; Viner 1937). Liberal arguments, like those predating liberalism, link the pacifying elements of trade to economic and sociological factors. Economic arguments permeate the contemporary liberal argument, but there is also an implicit (and at times explicit) assumption that the increased contact that results from trade ties promotes peace and unifies states. While related, the economic and sociological strands of liberalism rely on different dynamics to explain the trade-conflict relationship.

Perhaps the argument receiving the most scholarly attention in related literature suggests that states are deterred from initiating conflict against a trading partner for fear of losing the welfare gains associated with the trading relationship (Polachek 1980). Given the prominence of economic arguments seeking to explain the trade-peace connection, it is useful to begin with a discussion of a few key assumptions formulated from classical trade theory, where the rationale for the link between trade and interstate peace is established.[3] As will become apparent, theorists critical of the assumptions underlying classical trade theory are also the most ardent critics of the trade-peace proposition.

First, liberal economists believe trade provides benefits to its participants. They do not assume that the benefits of trade are equal for all actors, but they nevertheless assume these are positive. Liberals also assume that trade occurs voluntarily; therefore, if we see two actors trading, they are doing so because they are deriving benefits from the relationship; otherwise, as rational actors, they would exit the relationship. Thus, if we witness states engaging in trade, we must assume that they are deriving benefits. According to this argument, if a state did not enjoy net benefits from a particular relationship, being a rational actor, it would terminate the relationship. As we will see, neo-Marxist scholars reject the notion that the existence of trade ties signifies voluntary exchange.

Underlying neoclassical trade theory is the notion that states are better off if they trade than they would be if they refrained from trade. The gains from trade that neoclassical trade theory assumes accrue to states arise from the possibility of exchange and from greater specialization. Through exchange, states are able to sell and therefore purchase products at a lower price than if they were pursuing economic autarky. Exchange is assumed to increase revenue as well as consumption. More important, trade increases the productive efficiency of the economy through specialization. By specializing in those products for which a state has a relative advantage, it is better able to allocate resources to efficient productive ventures. According to this argument, economic specialization and trade increase real income, both nationally and globally.

Those who argue that trade fosters peace most often maintain that intense conflict is deterred when leaders consider the welfare losses associated with an interruption to trade. For most contemporary liberal theorists, it is not the act of trade itself, but the threat of losing the economic benefits of such ties that deters states from seeking military actions against their most important trading partners. Several authors provide empirical evidence of the negative relationship between trade and conflict and/or the positive relationship between trade and cooperation (e.g., Domke 1988; Gasiorowski and Polachek 1982; Oneal et al. 1996; Oneal and Ray 1997; Oneal and Russett 1997, 1999; Polachek 1980, 1992; Polachek and McDonald 1992; Polachek et al. 1997, 1999; Sayrs 1990).

Polachek's (1980) expected-utility model of trade and conflict provides a framework for understanding leaders' calculations of the relative costs and benefits of interstate trade and conflict. The model provides the basis for understanding the arguments of both advocates and critics of the proposition that trade promotes peace. The model has been utilized, criticized, and modified by theorists within and outside the liberal school of thought.[4] Operating within the framework of neoclassical trade theory, Polachek assumes that trade patterns emerge as a result of given heterogeneous factor endowments among nations. These trade patterns, and the accruing benefits associated with the gains from trade, affect a rational leader's foreign policy behavior, as she or he attempts to maximize social welfare. According to Polachek's model, in a leader's expected-utility calculus, the cost of conflict equals the lost welfare gains associated with potential trade losses (1980, 1992). Even if conflict does not lead to the cessation of trade, it will lead to inferior terms of trade, such as lower prices for exports or higher prices for imports (Polachek and McDonald 1992). The diminution of trade or barriers to trade that accompany conflict lead to welfare losses. Thus, increases in gains from trade in a particular relationship are believed to reduce incentives for conflict within that relationship. According to Polachek's model, the expansion of trade ties with a given state should reduce the likelihood of conflict.

A similar cost-benefit analysis is provided by those theorists who judge leaders' decisions by their assessment of the utility of pursuing trading versus military strategies for acquiring desired goods. Rosecrance (1986) argues that states pursue trading strategies when military options become too costly and less efficient relative to trade. This focus differs from Polachek's expected-utility model. Polachek's model suggests that once trade ties have been established, deterring conflict can only maximize welfare; that is, conflict only produces a negative effect on welfare in Polachek's model. For others, the cost-benefit analysis incorporates a consideration of trade versus conquest. Although liberal theorists assume that trade is the preferred strategy for acquiring resources, within the cost-benefit analysis of trade and conflict we can imagine instances in which the acquisition of resources through conflict remains a viable and at times more desirable option than trade, as suggested by the title of Liberman's 1996 book *Does Conquest Pay?* He finds support for the argument that conquest can pay under some conditions. Thus, the cost-benefit analysis for states' decisions to pursue trading versus military strategies to further the national interest may result in outcomes where the utility of conflict is greater than that for trade.[5] Although Rosecrance focuses on the system-level characteristics altering the trade-military calculus over time, from both his and Polachek's model we can assume that the utility of conflict relative to trade may also vary across space (e.g., across dyadic relationships).

An extended argument advanced by liberals regarding the trade-conflict relationship maintains that it is not merely the *volume* of trade, but also the *type* of trade existing between partners that affects utility calculations for conflict (Polachek 1980). For example, Polachek and McDonald (1992) stress the importance of measuring the elasticity of supply and demand for goods traded, providing evidence that the more inelastic an actor's import and export demand and supply to a target country, the smaller the amount of actor-to-target net conflict. States are believed to be more vulnerable relative to those whose products and purchases are in greater demand, particularly when the goods are of strategic importance. Unfortunately, it is difficult to measure the importance of different types of trade for a country, particularly if one wishes to focus on a broad historical and temporal domain. The strategic relevance of commodities changes over time, making it difficult to apply general measures of commodity importance. In addition, data for measuring the elasticity of trade are limited, so work in this area has been curtailed. Researchers generally rely on proxy measures of interdependence that assess the importance of a given relationship relative to others, rather than assessing whether the traded commodities themselves produce the dependence.

For some liberals, trade's pacifying effect results from more than economic considerations. Many eighteenth-century tracts by political economists expressed the view that commerce civilizes, polishes, and pacifies states and their citizens (Hirschman 1977, 1982). Montesquieu was among the first to cite the positive transformations that commerce brings to society (Forbes 1997). In 1749, he wrote "Commerce . . . polishes and softens . . . (adoucit) barbaric ways as we can see every day" (quoted in Hirschman 1982, 1464). Those who engaged in commerce were assumed to become more peaceful, more civilized. In 1781, Samuel Richard wrote:

> Commerce has a special character which distinguishes it from all other professions. It affects the feelings of men so strongly that it makes him who was proud and haughty suddenly turn supple, bending, and serviceable. Through commerce, man learns to deliberate, to

be honest, to acquire manners, to be prudent, and reserved in both talk and action. . . . he flees vice, or at least his demeanor exhibits decency and seriousness. (quoted in Hirschman 1982, 1465)

Some contemporary liberal analysts portray business interests as more pacific and antiwar than other elements of society (Domke 1988). However, contemporary arguments generally attribute business people's peacefulness to their economic interest, rather than adopting the classical view that commerce has transformed their character. The economic argument suggests that business interests will mobilize their opposition to war in the interest of maintaining trade ties (economic profits). Some liberals add that this is particularly true in democratic societies, where public opinion has a greater impact on policymakers (Domke 1988; Ray 1995). Alternatively, one might argue that in nondemocratic regimes, the power of the business class is even more enhanced relative to democratic regimes, where alternative groups have an equal opportunity to exert influence over foreign policy. This arrangement may be due to the nondemocratic state's reliance on powerful economic actors for subsidizing state objectives. However, the argument that business interests always prefer peace to conflict is countered easily by the many instances in which businesses profit from war or in which economic interests prefer conflict to peace (Barbieri and Levy 1999).

The positive social transformation arising from commerce is not only argued by classical liberals to affect the behavior of individuals, but is assumed to transform societies—to make them less warlike. In addition, liberals assume that commerce alters relationships between societies. In *The Spirit of the Laws* (1749) Montesquieu wrote that "commerce cures destructive prejudices" (quoted in Forbes 1997, 2). Greater contacts, according to this view, produce greater understanding and more peaceful unions. In addition, increased contact necessitates the creation of mechanisms, such as laws, to resolve conflicts of interest that might arise. Trade facilitates the creation of additional linkages that bind states together.

Liberals, functionalists, and neofunctionalists argue that the expansion of interstate linkages in one area stimulates further cooperation in other areas (Deutsch et al. 1957; Haas 1958, 1964; Mitrany 1964). Of course, the unity that arises from economic ties can be attributed to the self-interested desire to maintain economic benefits and/or to the presumed social attachments that arise from close contacts. The views are not unrelated, but there are some important distinctions. Liberals envision a world community arising from a global division of labor in which national boundaries could be weakened for the good of the community and its prosperity. Trade, even if pursued for economic gains, should lead to the unification of societies through a convergence of interests and cultures. According to this view, trade breaks down the barriers and prejudices associated with national identities. States and their citizens become integrated into one global community, united by a common interest. The increased contact and intermingling of cultures that exist between trading states are assumed to have a homogenizing effect. Again, a main premise is that contact and homogenization are good for peace, a view subject to support as well as criticism. In sum, contact is presumed to reduce misperceptions, increase understanding, lead to a convergence of cultures, foster formal and informal institutions to facilitate trade, and have spillover effects into other areas that lead to greater cooperation.

Thus, while liberals recognize that gains from trade and the potential costs accompanying interdependence are not always equal, they argue that trade ties generate net positive benefits for each state involved. These benefits are not solely economic. Rather, trade is seen as a positive force for transforming individuals, society, and relations between societies. Within the liberal tradition, a clear link is therefore established between expanded trade and peace. The expansion of trade ties alone should reduce the likelihood of conflict. This link of trade to peace, as we will see, is tenuous for those who maintain that trade might entail net costs, for those who view states' concerns about absolute gains as subordinate to concerns about relative gains, and for those who view increased contact as harmful to interstate relations.

Trade's Impact Is Contingent on the Nature of Dependence

Liberal theorists describe trading relationships as universally beneficial. They also differentiate relationships according to the extensiveness of trade ties, rather than the more general context in which trading relationships exist (e.g., in relations of unequal power). Critics of commercial liberalism argue that all economic relations are not created equal; some trading relationships may promote harmonious, beneficial interstate relations, while others are plagued by tension. Neo-Marxists reject the assumption that trade provides net benefits to all states. Trade and economic dependence benefit the powerful, but result in political and economic costs for the powerless. Dependency theorists reject the notion of universal voluntary exchange and argue that developing nations, as a result of historical-structural relationships, are not free actors and are therefore unable to make the same calculations proposed by the expected-utility models (Tétreault and Abel 1986). The existence of trade ties does not imply mutual benefits, but may instead reflect an absence of latitude on the part of some states to break free from undesirable trade relations. Neorealists contribute to the debate by adding that even when absolute gains exist, concerns about relative gains may dominate leaders' decisions (see Baldwin 1993; Grieco 1990; Mastanduno 1993; Powell 1991; Snidal 1991, 1993). Tensions may arise over how the gains from trade are distributed. Thus, trade may be devoid of the benefits and incentives presumed by liberals to serve as a restraint to conflict.

A reading of critical theories of trade leads one to infer that trade's impact on interstate relations is contingent upon the distribution of costs and benefits in a given relationship. In large part, the consequences of trade are contingent on whether dependence is symmetrical. Asymmetrical trade relations are more likely to produce disproportionate costs and benefits, where the more dependent state incurs greater costs and fewer benefits. These costs may be political, economic, or social. Asymmetrical dependence confers unequal power to the less dependent state. The advantaged bargaining position of the less dependent state may be used to gain concessions on economic or political issues (Hirschman [1945] 1980). Thus, one might hypothesize that tensions are more likely to arise in asymmetrical relations due to the exercise of power derived through such relations, the perception of negative consequences of dependence, or concerns about relative gains.

An eclectic group of theorists emphasizes the negative consequences of economic dependence (Balogh 1963; Cooper 1968; Emmanuel 1972; Gasiorowski 1986a, 1986b; Hirschman [1945] 1980; Kegley and Richardson 1980; Wallensteen 1973). Dependency theorists and neo-Marxists provide perhaps the most comprehensive assessment about the detrimental effects of economic dependence for a nation and its economic development (Amin 1977; Baran 1957; Cardoso and Faletto 1979; Evans 1979; Frank 1967; Furtado 1963; Myrdal 1957; Prebisch

1950; Seers 1963; Singer 1950).[6] In criticizing liberal assumptions about the universal benefits of free trade, dependency theorists argue: (1) the gains from trade are enjoyed exclusively by developed states; (2) trading relations between developed and developing nations retard the development process of developing states; and (3) trade exacerbates inequalities in the wealth of nations (Singer 1950; Myrdal 1957; Seers 1963). For Seers (1963) and others, underdevelopment results from relations between states, rather than internal conditions within developing nations. "Development for one of the parties will therefore tend to imply underdevelopment for the other, depending on their relative positions within the structure binding them together" (Blomström and Hettne 1984, 18). Frank (1967) views the "development of underdevelopment" as a result of economic dependence, while Cardoso maintains that growth might occur in the periphery, but it will entail "capitalist dependent development" (see Blomström and Hettne 1984, 67, 75).

The dependency school of thought focuses primarily on relations between developed and developing states, but the negative consequences of dependence may arise within other types of interstate relations. Marxist attention to the exploitative nature of unequal exchange relations, as well as realist views about the use of economic instruments for promoting power, illustrate the long tradition of skepticism about free trade. The views expressed by Max Sering mirror those arguments located in contemporary critiques of liberalism:

It ha[s] been wrongly contended that in the economic intercourse of nations the dependence is always a mutual one, that always equal values are exchanged. As between private persons, there exist between national economies relations of exploitation and of subjection. (1900, quoted in Hirschman [1945] 1980, 11)

In his seminal work, *National Power and the Structure of Foreign Trade,* Hirschman was among the first contemporary scholars to elaborate on "how relations of influence, dependence and domination arise right out of mutually beneficial trade" ([1945] 1980, vii). He states:

The Nazis . . . had not perverted the international economic system, they had merely capitalized on one of its potentialities or side effects; for "power elements and disequilibria are potentially inherent in such 'harmless' trade relations as have always taken place, e.g., between big and small, rich and poor, industrial and agricultural countries—relations that could be fully in accord with the principles taught by the theory of international trade." (vii)

Hirschman grounds his notion of dependence on the importance of one trading partner relative to others. When one state maintains most of its trade with a given partner and lacks the freedom to alter existing trade patterns, "dependence" results. Dependence arises from a state's inability to spread its imports and exports equally over a large number of countries. States with a limited set of trading partners are assumed to be more dependent on those with whom they trade heavily. In particular, when structural linkages exist, dependent states are less able to alter their trade patterns and may become subject to manipulation. The lack of freedom and the perpetuation of dependence preclude states from enjoying the benefits of trade as described by liberals, whose model did not show states subjected to the coercive political pressures found in relations of dependence.

Thus, a natural component of trade relations is the potential use of asymmetrical dependence as a method to exert political pressure on a trade partner. Unlike some critics of liberalism who reject the idea that all states benefit from trade, Hirschman accepts this view, but also underscores the potentially adverse consequences associated with these benefits. For liberals, the more dependent state, such as a developing nation, generally enjoys greater economic benefits from an opportunity to trade with a large state than the large state derives from the relationship. It is the dependent state's fear of losing the gains from trade that enables the less dependent (more powerful) state to enjoy a disproportionate amount of influence in the trading relationship. In turn, the leverage accruing to the more powerful state from this asymmetrical dependence may be used to gain concessions in either the political or economic domains. Thus, it is the less powerful state's desire to acquire and preserve the gains from trade that perpetuate relations of dependence and the consequences that entails.

In *Power and Interdependence,* Keohane and Nye (1977) build upon Hirschman's notion of how asymmetrical dependence serves as a source of power for the less dependent state. Although these works do not explicitly address the trade-conflict relationship, they illuminate the dynamics present in asymmetrical relations. The manipulation and potential for coercive tactics characteristic of asymmetrical relationships stand in sharp contrast to the harmonious ties described by liberals. This raises the question of whether asymmetrical dependence can ever be described as peaceful, or whether asymmetrical dependence is incongruent with the notion of peace.

Within the context of this study, I wish to assess the extent to which coercion manifests itself in explicit threats of violence. However, there are some theorists that might argue that the types of relationships involving asymmetrical dependence violate the notion of peace, by involving implicit threats and "structural violence" (Galtung 1971). What is clear is that the dynamics of asymmetrical dependence are likely to produce hostilities between actors, creating a predisposition for conflict. Still, it is equally plausible that the more powerful state has the ability to suppress conflict before it erupts, but that the types of tactics used to suppress dissent may in themselves constitute a violation of peace.

Control by the more powerful state is not confined to political or economic manipulation, but also may involve active military intervention. Wallensteen (1973) demonstrates that powerful states are more likely than minor powers to intervene militarily or engage in military confrontation with underdogs that are dependent upon them economically. For example, Wallensteen cites several instances in which the United States pursued military actions against Latin American states that were economically dependent upon the United States. Thus, Wallensteen shows that asymmetrical dependence not only threatens autonomy, but also can pose real threats to national security.

Although presumably more pronounced in asymmetrical relations, interdependence entails costs for mutually dependent states, as they become subject to the external influences of trading partners (Keohane and Nye 1977, 13). Even supporters of expanded trade ties recognize that extensive economic interdependence threatens national autonomy and poses problems for policymakers. As Cooper states:

Like other forms of international contact, international economic intercourse both enlarges and confines the freedom of countries to act according to their own lights. It enlarges their freedom by permitting a more economical use of limited resources; it confines their freedom by embedding each country in a matrix of constraints which it can influence only slightly, often only indirectly, and without certainty of effect. . . . As with a marriage, the benefits of close international economic relations can be enjoyed only at the expense of giving up a certain amount of national independence, or autonomy, in setting and pursuing economic objectives. (Cooper and Council on Foreign Relations 1968, 4)

States must resolve the dilemma of simultaneously reaping the benefits of interdependence without impeding their own national objectives. Cooper acknowledges that this is more difficult for smaller than for larger countries, since the former are forced to adjust their behavior to conform to the wishes of the states they are dependent upon (5). However, when Cooper employs the analogy of marriage to describe interdependent relationships between states he overlooks the intense forms of violence that too often manifest themselves in close relationships, such as those between spouses or lovers. Therefore, Cooper's perception of the negative consequences of interdependence and the ways in which states might overcome such adverse effects are very different from the harsher scenarios one might portray about interdependent relationships.

Trade dependence can limit autonomy beyond the economic realm. Kegley and Richardson (1980) specifically address the effect of economic dependence on foreign policy compliance, arguing that dependent trade partners are subject to the demands of the stronger trade partner when making foreign policy decisions. The influence effect of trade ties has been portrayed in a positive light by some advocates of trade expansion, who view "constructive engagement" as a means to alter the domestic and foreign policies of their trading partners. For example, many policymakers in the United States argue that the expansion of trade ties with China will provide an avenue for influencing the Chinese human rights record. Similarly, some Western policymakers consider trade to be a means to expose states to democratic systems and believe this will foster transitions to democracy. For others, the threat of severing trade ties (economic sanctions), rather than policies of constructive engagement, is preferred as a more subtle means of exerting coercive influence on trade partners than would be achieved by threats of force. In either case, trade is portrayed as an instrument to exert influence on other nations. The target of such influence attempts might then view trade ties as a challenge to their autonomy.

Gasiorowski (1986a, 1986b) and Kegley and Richardson (1980) show that the political impact of dependence and the negative consequences of trade are more pronounced in asymmetrical relations. Gasiorowski (1986a, 1986b) provides evidence that those countries that are more dependent on trade as a source of national income are more hostile toward countries on which they are interdependent. Economic interactions are only associated with declines in conflict when the costs of interdependence are minimized, as when states design policies to reduce potential threats to national autonomy (Cooper and Council on Foreign Relations 1968; Gasiorowski 1986a).

What is unclear in debates concerning economic dependence, particularly asymmetrical dependence, is whether the use of power derived from asymmetrical dependence is sufficient to create tensions necessary for the outbreak of militarized hostilities. Relations that fail to provide mutual benefits or impose disproportionate costs on one actor may be characterized as hostile, without manifesting themselves in military conflicts. Hostilities might be suppressed when states see some benefit in preserving the relationship or when states fear more costly reprisals from breaking ties with dominant states. Russett notes that "conflict may be suppressed by the operation of a relationship where one party dominates the other" (1967, 192). It is plausible to argue that the power dynamics that characterize asymmetrical relations create a predisposition for conflict greater than that found in symmetrical trade relations. Yet, whether such hostilities manifest themselves in conflict remains an empirical question.

The pacifying influence of trade may also give way to discord when one state believes that its partner is enjoying disproportionate benefits within the relationship. Neorealists' focus on relative gains provides a basis for understanding why the presence of absolute gains may neither be sufficient to satisfy states nor create a disincentive to conflict. Although concerns about relative gains are not limited to asymmetric relations, there may be greater concerns about relative gains, since the costs and benefits in asymmetrical relations may be more pronounced in such relationships compared to those that are more balanced. Even when states are thought to benefit absolutely from trade, one state might consider its partner's disproportionate gain to be a loss to itself in terms of relative power. This is particularly the case when trading relations possess characteristics of cooperation as well as competition. For example, trading relations between the United States and Japan exemplify a contemporary case of the tensions that erupt over relative gains. Most liberal economists would argue that the United States and Japan both derive net benefits from their trading relationship, but we frequently see that concerns over relative gains often dominate trade disputes. R. G. Hawtry provides important insight into the sources of tensions that may arise over relative gains:

> So long as welfare is the end, different communities may cooperate happily together. Jealousy there may be and disputes as to how that material means of welfare should be shared. But there is no inherent divergence of aim in the pursuit of welfare. Power, on the other hand, is relative. The gain of one country is necessarily loss to others, its loss is gain to them. Conflict is the essence of the pursuit of power. (1930, quoted in Hirschman [1945] 1980, 27)

The relevance of relative gains to trading relationships is highlighted in the work of Gowa (1994). Gowa assesses the security externalities associated with trade and argues that states choose to trade with allies in order to avoid granting the gain from trade to adversaries, which results in security externalities. She argues that it is not the increased income that is of greatest concern in trade with an adversary, but the ability of the adversary to enjoy the gains arising from specialization. Permitting an adversary the opportunity to increase its productive efficiency and redirect resources away from alternative productive ventures could allow it to increase production of military resources, which would pose a potential challenge.

The relative-gain argument depicts one state's gain in trade as being another state's potential loss. This characterization of trade is made more explicit in Marxist arguments about the structure of unequal exchange relations. For example, some neo-Marxists argue that trade between developed and developing nations siphons off resources from the poor to the rich state (see Galtung 1971). In this scenario, poor states have little power to break free from exploitative trade relations, particularly when the legacy of colonialism and neoimperialism have left poor states structurally linked to the dominant states. As noted earlier, liberals maintain that smaller states enjoy disproportionate benefits in their trading relations with large states. Whether one accepts the liberal economist or Marxist interpretation of who benefits more in relations between developing and developed states, it is clear that perceptions about the distribution of benefits might affect one's assessment of trading relations, in both theory and practice, and that perceptions seem to differ depending upon the type of trading relationship that exists. And it is perception, as well as objective reality, that creates tensions and shapes leaders' decisions to engage in conflict.

Trade Increases Conflict

A third group of theorists rejects the notion that international trade provides an impetus to peace. Although lacking a unified position, several systemic theories grounded in Marxist-Leninist or resource-scarcity perspectives predict greater conflict accompanying the expansion of trade. A similar view is expressed in the neorealist writings of Kenneth Waltz (1979), who argues that increased interdependence at the system level leads to increased conflict. His rationale, shared by critics of the contact hypothesis, is that increased contact creates potential opportunities for discord.

Within the tradition of Lenin's theory of imperialism, neo-Marxists view competition over markets and resources as an inherent feature of capitalism (Baran 1957; Sweezy 1942). This competition can easily result in violent conflict between major powers, as well as the domination of less powerful states. Lateral pressure theory also envisions conflict corresponding with shortages of resources and markets (Choucri and North 1975, 1989). Similarly, neomercantilist theories anticipate greater conflict emerging when states pursue aggressive policies for capitalist expansion under the guise of the national interest. When such behavior emerges among major powers, the result can be trade wars, investment wars, or even hegemonic wars (Sayrs 1990).

Theories maintaining that conflict is inherently related to exchange relations primarily originate as outgrowths of Marx's ([1887] 1906) notion that capitalism is exploitative in its very nature and results in conflict between classes, as well as between factions of capital. In fact, Marx favored free trade, rather than protectionism, because he felt free trade would create tensions that would accelerate the inevitable crisis and inevitable demise of capitalism (see Marx 1848). Similarly, Lenin's theory of imperialism is grounded in the aggressive nature of monopoly capitalism, whereby conflict is an integral part of capitalist expansion. Hobson rejected the notion that capitalism itself was responsible for aggressive expansionism, arguing instead that imperialism is the result of capitalism's maladjustment ([1902] 1954).

Rosecrance (1986) provides a useful distinction between Marxist-Leninist and dependency theories in terms of their predictions about the impact of trade on international conflict. He notes that dependency theories assume a degree of collusion among developed capitalist states with conflict arising in relations between unequal partners. Lenin, however, argues that the highest stage of capitalist development—imperialism—leads to conflict among the most advanced capitalist nations as they vie for control over new markets, sources of raw materials, and scarce resources. But Rosecrance's distinction may not capture the full flavor of Lenin's theory. Lenin clearly sees capitalist states vying for control over less powerful states. In the process, capitalist states employ force to gain control over desired territories and to subjugate the inhabitants of these territories.

Although insightful, theories of imperialism and resource scarcity at the system level are less helpful in developing hypotheses at the dyadic level. Hypotheses related to imperialism may actually be more applicable to triadic-level analysis. That is, the most intense conflicts arise from capitalist competition between states vying for control over a third state. Thus, the conflicting states are not themselves interdependent, but seek to establish relations of dependence and domination with the same third party. Although not the subject of this study, theories of imperialism highlight the potential problems in assuming that the expansion of trade will always have pacifying effects on conflict. More important, if we wish to predict where conflict is most likely to occur between economic partners, two competing hypotheses emerge. Conflict between powerful nations may be the central concern, but conflict between asymmetrical partners is also likely, since powerful nations may use force or other coercive means to gain territory and markets in weaker nations or to establish and maintain relations of dependence. In general, critical theories provide a picture of trading relationships that stands in sharp contrast to the harmonious ones portrayed by liberals.

Just as theorists differ over the economic interpretations of trade's impact, scholars disagree about whether close contact through commerce or other ties is beneficial for fostering peace. As noted, Waltz (1979) maintains that increased interdependence creates more opportunities for conflict. Forbes (1997) reviews a large body of theoretical and empirical literature relevant to the contact hypothesis (that contact has a positive effect on relations between individuals and societies, and close contact serves to break down prejudices between people and nations and to foster peaceful relations). The majority of the empirical evidence reviewed suggests that contact between individuals reduces prejudices and improves relationships, but increased contact between aggregate groups such as nations appears to be correlated with conflict. His review of contact theory highlights the need to distinguish between different types of contact. Theorists differ over which types of contact are good and which are bad for producing peaceful integration. I would argue that those situations in which actors believe they derive benefits from contact are more likely to produce desirable effects, while those in which actors believe they do not benefit are likely to increase conflict. What appears clear is that not all economic relationships, or all contacts, produce the same effect.

Trade Has an Insignificant or
Counterbalancing Effect on Conflict

Realist literature suggests that the influence of trade is subordinate to other considerations in determining the incidence of international conflict (Blainey 1973; Blanchard and Ripsman 1994; Bueno de Mesquita 1981; Buzan 1984; Levy 1989; Ripsman and Blanchard 1996/97). Realist theorists have traditionally relegated economic concerns to the domain of "low politics," elevating concerns about national security to the central focus in international relations scholarship. Neoliberals argue that the traditional hierarchy of issues advanced by realist scholars is no longer viable as a framework for studying an interdependent world (Keohane and Nye 1977). Still, economic considerations remain subordinate to military concerns in realist assessments of leaders' decisions to engage in conflict. According to realist logic, trade will not create a sufficient deterrent to conflict. This does not mean that trade ties are unimportant for realists. Trade is recognized as a tool of influence. Trading relationships with states that provide strategic commodities are also valued. However, when faced with questions about whether to engage in conflict, leaders do not necessarily evaluate the potential harm that might be caused to a trading relationship.

Finally, it may be that there are enough instances in which trading relationships are conflictual and in which they are cooperative that the two sets of cases cancel each other out. Trade may, in fact, matter in some relationships, but not in others. Trade may also contribute to conflict and to peace and do so in a manner where the examples one finds of either set of cases balance against each other. We would therefore observe a null finding—that there is no relationship, on average, between trade and conflict. The statistical result of such a situation would be akin to the conclusions made by those who say that trade is irrelevant to conflict. In the case of canceling out, trade may be very relevant, but the directional influence varies in too many instances to find one dominant pattern.

CONSOLIDATING ALTERNATIVE
PROPOSITIONS

One way to reconcile the differences in the propositions advanced by alternative theoretical traditions is to consider the commonalities among various arguments. The basis of trade's pacifying effect is presumed to arise from the benefits derived from economic linkages. When such ties are believed to contribute to poverty or domestic disequilibria, the pacifying influence of trade may be neutralized. In fact, it may be reversed, whereby increased trade leads to increased conflict. Although not considered in relation to trade and conflict, Russett (1983) emphasizes the important link between poverty and conflict, and peace and prosperity. Describing the potential for violence that may result during times of economic crisis, Russett's analysis has implications for the research question at hand: for if one state perceives poverty to arise from economic relations, trading relations might become hostile; whereas when states enjoy increased prosperity from trade, trading relations might become harmonious. Similarly, Neff (1990) notes that economic nationalism tends to resurface during periods of economic recession, while free trade flourishes during periods of prosperity. In sum, beneficial trade may deter conflict, while situations characterized by disproportionate detrimental effects from trade might be associated with conflict.

Accepting the liberal premise that the gains from trade provide a disincentive to conflict, one would anticipate states refraining from engaging in conflict with their most important trading partners. While reasonable, it is apparent that the notion that trade promotes peace is only one of a number of alternative hypotheses. It is possible to envision instances in which the benefits to be gained from conflict exceed those to be gained from the preservation of the trading relationship. One can also imagine instances in which asymmetrical dependence may give rise to conflicts or, at a minimum, fail to inhibit them. Given the aforementioned theoretical propositions, it is clear that a case can be made for the promotion of peace through trade; conflict as a product of trade; or trade having no effect on interstate conflict. Moreover, trade's impact on conflict may be contingent upon the nature of dependence in the relationship, whereby symmetrical ties may promote peace, but asymmetrical ties exacerbate conflict. This suggests that trade's impact on interstate relations is variable.

I evaluate the relative validity of each proposition relevant to the trade-conflict relationship. Several theorists offer clues about the types of trading relations that are most likely to produce mutual benefits and therefore possess the greatest potential for fostering peace. Theorists also provide clues about the conditions most likely to stimulate contempt in economic relationships, suggesting which dyads are less likely to enjoy the pacifying influence of trade.

To evaluate alternative propositions about the trade—conflict relationship, it is important to identify relationships hypothesized to promote peace. Liberals, for example, highlight the importance of extensive trade ties for reducing conflict. The balance of dependence is irrelevant to the liberal proposition that trade promotes peace. Theories critical of liberalism stress the variations that exist across economic relationships, where the symmetrical nature of dependence is an important element is assessing the consequences of trade ties. As mentioned in chapter 1, interdependence generally implies relations of mutual need and, by extension, mutual vulnerability between actors, while dependence connotes asymmetrical relations. Keohane and Nye (1977, 8–9) make a further distinction between interdependence and interconnectedness, where interconnectedness represents weak linkages among states.

Rather than thinking about the presence or absence of interdependence and dependence as a strict dichotomy, I conceptualize trade relations along a continuum, where characteristics of different types of relationships may coexist. Relations of dependence, where one state is heavily dependent on the relationship and the other lacks dependence, are generally considered in related literature to be the most conflictual (Hirschman [1945] 1980). Relations characterized by mutual need seem to entail less costly dimensions to the relationship.

It is useful to provide a graphic representation that simplifies the relationship between interdependent, dependent, and relatively independent

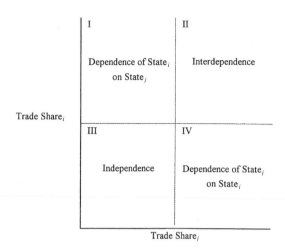

FIG. 1. Dependence and interdependence continuum

relations. Figure 1 represents a dyadic relationship, where each axis measures the trade share each state has of its partner's total trade. Quadrants I and IV represent scenarios in which one state is disproportionately dependent upon the other partner, considered by critics of liberalism to be the most conflictual. Quadrants II and III represent conditions of mutual (symmetrical) dependence, yet in the latter case dependence is minimal. Thus, dyads falling within quadrant III have symmetrical, but not salient economic relations. To distinguish between the balance and the extent of dependence, imagine a line bisecting the origin at a 45-degree angle and extending out to the point where each state has 100 percent of its trade with one partner. The closer dyads fall to this diagonal line, the more *balanced* the relationship. For some theorists, symmetry is the most important factor for fostering peace in a relationship regardless of the extent of such ties.[7] For other states, relations falling within lower ranges of the line (i.e., in quadrant III) lack the bonds sufficient to inhibit conflict. Taken as a whole, the various scenarios described by alternative schools of thought would suggest that relations that have both extensive and balanced trade dependence offer the greatest hope for peace (i.e., those trading relationships falling within quadrant II).

This figure is useful in considering ways in which we can capture alternative types of trading relationships. Moreover, we may do this with an eye toward considering the concerns of liberals and their critics. This will be useful when we consider how best to create measures that capture the types of relationships portrayed in alternative theoretical scenarios about the trade-conflict relationship. That will be a primary goal in the next chapter.

CONCLUSION

My review of the literature reveals highly diverse views about the impact of economic ties on interstate relations. From liberal theory, one would conclude that trade has an inverse effect on interstate conflict; the more important a trading relationship, the less likely a pair of states will be to engage in conflict. Neo-Marxist theories suggest that the impact on conflict is dependent upon the balance of dependence, where symmetry of dependence may inhibit conflict, but asymmetry may exacerbate conflict. Finally, within the realist tradition, trade relations are thought to have little influence on leaders' decisions to engage in or refrain from conflict. In the next chapter, I analyze these alternative propositions regarding the trade-conflict relationship.

Chapter 3

INVESTIGATING THE

COMMERCIAL PEACE

The theories presented in chapter 2 suggest a number of competing propositions about the trade-conflict relationship. Scholars have begun to apply social-scientific techniques to investigating the relative accuracy of these alternative portrayals of the trade-conflict relationship. However, the evidence produced from such efforts remains limited and mixed. This is, in part, a product of the differing approaches that scholars adopt to investigate the trade-conflict relationship. For example, scholars with alternative conceptions of trade and interdependence may choose to focus their attention in different areas, employing different explanatory models, different samples, and different measures of key constructs. Thus, differing findings within the literature should be understandable.

This chapter seeks to overcome some of the problems posed in previous research by setting forth a strategy for evaluating competing propositions about the trade-conflict relationship. The first section discusses previous efforts to assess empirically the impact of trade on conflict. Next, some of the main problems confronting trade-conflict researchers and a strategy to address some of these constraints are outlined. Then, I turn to my own empirical investigation of the trade-conflict relationship and discuss findings that are germane.

GAPS IN OUR KNOWLEDGE

Regardless of the perspective from which one approaches the trade-conflict debate, a litany of precedents exists to support one's position. Proponents of the argument that trade and other interstate linkages foster peace cite World War II as the primary example of the dangers inherent in rampant policies of protectionism. Liberals point to the intense economic rivalry, high protectionism, and economic instability that characterized the pre–World War II era and argue that the adverse economic impact of protectionism and the lack of incentives to deter conflict between states were root causes of the inability of states to stem the tide of that war. On the other hand, theorists who maintain that trade fails to prevent conflict or that interdependence may increase conflict point to the high level of economic interdependence that existed among European states on the eve of World War I. Although World Wars I and II are the most prominent examples employed in debates about the pacifying or conflictual aspects of economic relationships, a long list of other cases can be identified in which trading states either engage in or refrain from conflict. While interesting, anecdotal cases relevant to the trade-conflict relationship reveal no discernible pattern; one can easily identify cases of positive, negative, and insignificant relationships between trade and conflict.

For that reason, scholars have sought to identify systematically the factors associated with interstate conflict and cooperation.[1] Until recently, economic linkages were largely ignored in the literature devoted to the scientific study of conflict. As a consequence, only a partial picture of the connection between interdependence and conflict is furnished by the literature. Much of the research remains theoretical and anecdotal, with the majority of empirical studies being confined to limited samples of trading relationships. This study's purpose is to analyze a spatially and temporally broader domain than undertaken in previous research, in order to expand our understanding of the range of trading relationships that exist in the world. I hope to complement extensive historical studies of conflict in which economic linkages are absent altogether from the analysis, confined to a limited spatial or temporal domain, or investigated at an alternative level of analysis. My intent here is not to develop a comprehensive multicausal model of conflict, but rather to reveal how economic linkages may constitute an important piece of the conflict puzzle.

Researchers investigating the liberal proposition that trade promotes peace do so from a variety of theoretical and methodological approaches. Barbieri and Schneider (1999) provide a summary of quantitative studies that assess the impact of trade on conflict. This summary, which appears in table 1, indicates the diversity of measures, samples, analytical techniques, and findings among trade-conflict studies. Even scholars who appear to adopt similar research strategies often reach different conclusions about trade's ability to promote peace. Relative to other areas of conflict studies, research on the trade-conflict relationship is limited.

Until recently, historical studies of trade and conflict focused primarily on the system level of analysis, with the exception of Domke's (1988) monadic-level study. System-level studies have failed to achieve a consensus regarding the impact of economic interdependence on interstate conflict. Several of these studies (including Domke 1988, Rosecrance 1986, and Mansfield 1994) provide evidence that the expansion of trade over time has resulted in a general reduction in intensive forms of interstate conflict, whereas Waltz (1979), in his system-level analysis, argues that the decrease in interdependence during the post–World War II period is one of a set of factors contributing to peace in that era. Despite the lack of consensus across these studies, system-level research informs our understanding about the major trends and consequences of global interdependence. Yet, the extant literature provides very little information about variations that exist across relationships within the global system. Just as systemic interdependence varies across historical periods, with differing consequences for interstate relations, interdependence also varies in degree and character across pairs of states. Even within an interdependent world, some states may engage in war. The question posed here is whether states are more likely to engage in war with important trading partners or against those states with which they fail to trade.

To answer this question, it is important look within the system—at relations between states. Dyadic-level studies can address the question of who engages in conflict with whom. These studies, however, have been largely confined to the post–World War II era, a period that some consider unique in terms of the proliferation of international regimes and system characteristics that may be more conducive to the maintenance of harmonious trading relations. Blainey's (1973, chap. 2) proposition that what we consider a cause of peace may actually be the effect of peace may apply to the trade-conflict relationship in the post–World War II period—the expansion of trade may be the product and not the cause of peaceful relations between states.[2]

Several dyadic-level studies provide empirical support for the notion that trade promotes peace (Gasiorowski 1986a, 1986b; Gasiorowski and Polachek 1982; Oneal et al. 1996; Oneal and Ray 1997; Oneal and Russett 1997; Polachek 1980; Polachek et al. 1999; Polachek and McDonald 1992; and Sayrs 1990).[3] But these studies are all confined to the post–World War II period, and the majority focus on a limited spatial domain. Many focus exclusively on a subset of states referred to as "politically relevant" dyads: pairs of states that are contiguous or contain a major-power state (Oneal et al. 1996; Oneal and Ray 1997; Oneal and Russett 1997).

Even at the dyadic level, the empirical findings are mixed. Wallen-

TABLE 1. SUMMARY OF STATISTICAL STUDIES OF THE TRADE-CONFLICT RELATIONSHIP

Author(s)	Temporal Domain and Unit of Analysis	Methodological Techniques	Control Variables	Main Findings
Russett (1967)	1946–1965 41 warring dyads	Factor analysis Contingency tables		Trade to war [+]
Wallensteen (1973)	1920–1968 144 warring dyads	Contingency tables		Trade to war [+]
Polachek (1980)	1958–1967 dyads (30 states)	Regression, two staged LS	14 NAs	Trade to net conflict [–]
Gasiorowski and Polachek (1982)	1967–1978 US–Warsaw Pact	Regression Granger causality		Trade to net conflict [–]
Gasiorowski (1986a)	1948–1977 dyads (130 states)	Regression	PE, GDP	Mixed
Domke (1988)	1871–1975 states	Probit		Mixed
Polachek and McDonald (1992)	1973 dyads (14 OECD states)	Regression	PE, GDP	Trade to net conflict [–]
Polachek (1992)	1948–1978 dyads	Regression	DE, NA	Trade to net conflict [–]
Polachek (1997)	1948–1978 dyads (11 states)	Regression Three staged LS	17 NAs	Trade to net conflict [–]
	1958–1967 dyads (30 states)		RT	Trade to democratic peace [+]

Study	Time period	Method	Variables	Findings
Oneal et al. (1996)	1950–1985 PRD	Logit	A, EG, C, G, RT	Interdependence to MIDs [–]
Oneal and Ray (1997)	1950–1985 PRD	Logit	A, C, EG, G, RP, RT	Interdependence to MIDs [–]
Oneal and Russett (1997)	1950–1985 PRD	Logit	A, C, EG, GP, PC, RP, RT	Interdependence to MIDs [–]
Oneal and Russett (1999)	dyads	Logit	A, C, EG, GP, PC, R, RP	Interdependence to MIDs [–]
Barbieri (1995)	1870–1985 dyads	Logit	A, C, PR, RP	Interdependence to MIDs and wars [+]
Barbieri (1996a)	1870–1938 dyads	Logit	A, C, RT, RP	Interdependence to MIDs [+]
Barbieri (1997)	1870–1985 dyads	Logit	A, C, RT, RP	Interdependence to MIDs [+]
Mansfield (1994)	1850–1964 system	Regression	Con, EO, H	Trade to MP war [–] Openness to war [+]

Source: Reprinted from Barbieri and Schneider 1999, 395 (table II).

Key: A = Alliance ties; C = Contiguity; Con = Concentration of power; DE = Defense expenditure; EG = Economic growth; EO = Economic openness; GP = Geographic proximity; H = Hegemony; NA = National attributes (social-economic and demographic variables); PC = Political change; PE = Price elasticities; PR = Political relevance; PRD = "Politically relevant" dyads; RT = Regime type; RP = Relative power; TD = Temporal dependence.

steen (1973) and my own work provide evidence of the conflictual nature of interdependent relationships.[4] These analyses include a more comprehensive temporal and spatial domain than those found in dyadic studies that support the trade-promotes-peace hypothesis and are therefore more generalizable to a diverse group of trading relationships.

One might conclude that the variation in empirical findings in dyadic-level studies could be attributed to the period being investigated. However, as I reveal shortly, my investigation reveals no variations in the trade-conflict relationship across historical periods. Whether or not one accepts the argument that the post–World War II period is unique, it is important to determine empirically whether the trade-conflict relationship in this period is generalizable to other periods. For the characteristics that define the post–Cold War era and relations within the evolving interstate system may be more reminiscent of earlier periods of history. Thus, to understand what the future may hold for interdependent relations, it is useful to begin with an examination of the past. Does the proposition that trade promotes peace transcend time and space?

In addition, we might ask ourselves whether the propositions concerning the trade-conflict relationship are equally applicable to various levels of analysis (i.e., individuals, classes, states, and systems).[5] In some cases, the theories describing the trade-conflict relationship are more easily analyzed at one particular level of analysis, but the theories described in this study are generally framed in a manner that implies that they are equally applicable across levels of analysis. For example, liberals portray the benefits of trade as operating in interpersonal relations as well as international relations. Neo-Marxists have applied Marxian descriptions of the conflict inherent to interclass relations to those operating between states. This study focuses primarily on relationships between pairs of states, but it is informed by assumptions about economic relationships cast at different levels of analysis. Similarly, this investigation should advance our understanding about interdependence between actors at various levels of analysis.

RESEARCH STRATEGY

One of my main goals is to assess the empirical accuracy and generalizability of the competing views about trade's effect on peace. To do so requires analysis of a broader set of relationships than has previously been examined, to better consider those factors that might account for variations in the trade-conflict relationship. My focus of inquiry resides on dyadic interstate relationships, or pairs of states.[6] I wish to evaluate whether states behave differently toward other states, depending upon the degree of economic ties between them. This is a different question than asking whether trading states are more pacific than others or whether the international system is more peaceful during periods of high economic interdependence than low interdependence (see chap. 5).

The dyadic relationships included in my analyses vary with respect to the constituent states' national attributes, including economic, political, geographic, demographic, and ethnic characteristics. My criterion for including dyads in the study is grounded in the availability of data for the states comprising the dyad and for dyadic interactions. The study includes the period 1870–1992. In some instances the variables that I employ in my analyses necessitate that the particular tests be restricted to the post–World War II period.

For each dyad-year, values are recorded for the dependent variable at time t and for the explanatory variables at time $t-1$ (i.e., a one-year lag is introduced for all the independent variables). I employ lagged independent variables in order to reduce the problems posed by the reciprocal nature of the trade-conflict relationship. In fact, most researchers seem to believe that trade not only affects conflict, but also that conflict affects trade. Scholars differ in assessing the relative strength of these relationships. While further study is needed on this question, I choose to focus my inquiry here on the impact of trade on conflict, having found that relationship to be stronger than that of conflict on trade.

Although one of my key objectives in this study is to expand my domain of inquiry beyond that of others in order to assess the generalizability of the trade-promotes-peace proposition, data limitations pose barriers to the cases that I might analyze. For example, data availability is highly correlated with the level of development of a nation, particularly in the nineteenth century. This results in an inherent bias toward the disproportionate inclusion of developed states in the sample. I sought to overcome this bias by compiling data allowing me to produce a sample more closely reflective of the population of possible dyadic relationships present in the interstate system.[7] In addition, trade data, which are central to this investigation, contain their own set of problems. One problem is that these data are inherently biased in favor of states with important trading relationships, because data for a given state's top trading partners are more frequently reported in distinct categories than in cases of minor trading partners. Generally, the values of trade for minor trading partners are reported in an aggregated category labeled "all other countries." Data are unavailable about which states fall within this category. Thus, it is impossible to determine from most data sources whether two states refrained from trade or simply carried on a relatively limited share of trade. Some researchers choose to treat missing trade values as representative of zero trade ties between states, but I believe that such an assumption is false in many cases.

While some might consider minor trade flows to be similar to zero trade flows from a statistical perspective, there is certainly an important conceptual difference between states that have minor trade ties and those who have no trade. The absence of trade ties may indicate an absence of contact between states. Since contact is a necessary, but not sufficient, condition for conflict, it would be useful if we could determine whether states engaged in a minimum amount of trade, rather than no trade whatsoever. Unfortunately, this is not always possible. In the absence of detailed reports about a given trading relationship, I adopted the following coding rule. For the pre–World War II period, the absence of a trade-flow report with a given country was treated as a missing value. For the post–World War II period, almost all zero values were treated as missing. However, there were some cases where one state reports trading flows as being present and the other has a missing value. In such cases, some minor trade flows are treated as zero trade values when at least one state's trade report indicates that trade takes place between these states, since the International Monetary Fund (1991) maintains a minimum trade value reporting standard and treats values below a certain minimum threshold as zero trade.[8]

The Dependent Variable:
Militarized Interstate Disputes

In examining whether trade promotes peace, scholars differ in their conception of what a peaceful relationship entails and of what constitutes a violation of peace. For example, some may assume that peace exists when no war is present (Domke 1988). However, the absence of war alone is a very narrow definition of the type of relationship most people would accept as peaceful. For some scholars, high levels of cooperation signify peace, despite the fact that threats of violence and violent acts themselves may be present in a given relationship. In my own mind, peace entails more than just increased goodwill between actors. It involves refraining from threats and uses of force. Interdependent actors may engage in conflictual and cooperative behaviors (Azar and Eckhart 1978; Coser 1956; Hower 1990; Simmel 1955). Is it legitimate to describe a relationship as peaceful when actors resort to threats of violence, even if those threats are followed by gestures of cooperation? I assume that peace, at a minimum, should entail a commitment to refrain from violent behavior or threats to use violence. For this reason, I conceptualize peace as *the absence of militarized conflict,* rather than the presence of cooperation.

This distinction is an important one, since some empirical studies of the trade-conflict relationship combine cooperative and conflictual behaviors into an aggregate measure of "net conflict" (see Sayrs 1990; Polachek 1980).[9] In so doing, the general or aggregated characterization of the relationship might mask the violence present in the relationship. I assume that a peaceful relationship should be free from acts of military force short of war, including the threat to employ force. This does not mean that two or more actors have a perfect harmony of interests. Instead, it means that when conflicts of interest arise, nonviolent strategies are employed to resolve them.

In this study, I do not assume that the conflicts that arise between states are necessarily related to trade or other economic issues. In this respect, my investigation differs from those studies that focus on the economic causes of war (e.g., Richardson 1960, chap. 7). I do, however, assume that trade ties should affect the manner in which conflicts are resolved. If the trade-promotes-peace hypothesis is accurate, then interdependence should *condition* the means by which states resolve their conflicts of interest, regardless of the issue of dispute. For example, a state may have the capacity to use military force to win concessions in a particular interstate disagreement, but presumably would refrain from doing so against a state with whom it has strong ties. At its base, the relevant question here is whether the pacifying influence of trade is capable of defusing the desire to employ force when conflicts of interest arise between states.

Relationships characterized as peaceful should entail a different dynamic of conflict resolution than relationships described as hostile. We would not expect actors engaged in peaceful relationships to resort to threats of violence to get a friendly state to comply with their wishes. If anything, rewards are probably the strategy of choice for achieving compliance in a friendly relationship, while punishments are used in hostile relationships to compel another state to alter its behavior. This is, of course, an empirical question, and beyond the scope of this study. It does suggest, however, that trade may be part of an overall package of behaviors between friendly states. The methods a state employs to achieve compliance when a conflict of interest arises are determined, in part, by the overarching relationship between states. Similarly, a state's willingness to comply or compromise is partly dependent upon its relationship to the state issuing the demand. With respect to the methods used to achieve compliance, liberals assume that the bond between economic partners should make military strategies less likely. In addition, within interdependent relations, a state's willingness to conform to another state's demands should emerge from peaceful negotiations, a desire to continue harmonious relationships, or some sense of mutual obligation between partners. In short, truly peaceful interstate relationships should never involve using or threatening to use force in order to compel another state to alter its behavior.

Scholars engaged in the quantitative study of the trade-conflict relationship primarily rely on the Correlates of War revised Militarized Interstate Dispute (MID) data set (Jones, Bremer, and Singer 1996) to measure peace in a given relationship as the absence of militarized conflict between states. A MID is defined as "a set of interactions between or among states involving threats to use military force, displays of military force, or actual uses of military force" (Gochman and Maoz 1984, 586).[10] The MID data set permits researchers to measure the occurrence of MIDs, as well as several characteristics of these events. In this chapter, I examine whether pairs of states that are highly interdependent upon each other are less likely than others to engage in militarized interstate disputes. In the next chapter, I evaluate trade's impact on several characteristics of disputes beyond the onset of the conflict. This includes investigating whether the extent of a state's economic ties seems to influence the characteristics of military conflict, including whether interdependent states are more or less likely than others to prevent conflicts from escalating and are more likely to achieve negotiated settlements to conflict. Below, I account for the involvement of pairs of states in serious disputes. I sort yearly observations of dyads in the international system into two categories. The first category will consist of all those years in which a dyad experiences an outbreak of a MID (coded with a value of one). The second category consists of all those years in which the pair was not involved in a dispute (coded with a value of zero).[11] Multiple-party disputes are disaggregated into the constituent parties on each side of the conflict to reflect the dyadic nature of the study, whereby dyads composed of states on opposite sides of the conflict are coded as experiencing a dispute. MIDs are coded as such for the first year in which they occur; that is, multiple-year disputes are coded only once for a particular dyad. I adopt this rule, since the analytical technique that I employ in this study, logit regression, assumes that the events being analyzed are independent of each other.

The Independent Variables: Conceptualizing and
Operationalizing Interdependence

The primary difficulty in operationalizing trade and interdependence arises from the lack of a clear consensus about what these concepts are intended to capture. Given the differences in our theoretical conceptions of the trade-conflict relationship, researchers should not be surprised if we construct different operationalizations of the key variables central to our analysis. The theories that guide our analyses lack the necessary degree of specificity to facilitate a consensus about the most appropriate way to measure trade and interdependence, and the best strategy to analyze their impact on conflict. Theoretical ambiguities leave many things open for individual interpretation and yield countless possibilities for measurement construction. Even theorists who have similar theoretical conceptualizations of interdependence differ in how they prefer to measure the concept.

Scholars engaged in trade-conflict research might benefit from taking a closer look at the efforts of integration and dependency theorists who decades ago dealt with the same types of issues we confront today. Within each of these research programs, researchers employed a number of alternative operational measures of the phenomenon they wished to capture, whether integration or dependence. For example, Hirsch identifies more than sixteen operationalizations of trade dependence used in two decades of dependency literature (1986, 117). Since the time of his review, researchers have introduced new measures of dependence and interdependence and continue to do so, making it difficult to compare empirical findings across studies. Researchers appear to have made few advances in measurement construction from that which existed decades ago. While not ideal, having numerous measures of interdependence seems far less problematic than having one measure that does not fit our conceptualization of the phenomenon. But having so many measures makes it difficult to compare empirical findings and to accumulate knowledge. We have not thought enough about what different measures might be telling us, particularly when they yield alternative findings.

For example, Hughes's (1971) assessment of three common measures of integration seems timely for those contemplating which measures are most suitable for assessing the trade-conflict relationship. He analyzes the Savage and Deutsch (1957) null model, the export percentage model (exports/total exports), and the gross national product model (exports/GNP). Hughes argues that these are all reasonable measures, but adds that they may produce different findings. He believes that the way a researcher opts to introduce the size control for trade relative to either total transactions or total income can be traced to their notion of whether they believe integration is a constant sum or variable sum process. For the first two models, an increase in trade with one state must lead to a concurrent decline in integration with other states, since total trade represents, figuratively speaking, a pie being divided among partners. When GNP is used as a control for dyadic trade flows, integration can grow over time with all partners (i.e., if GNP is also growing). For interdependence, the growth in trade with one partner would signify a decline in dependence on all other states, if one were using total trade to reflect the importance of dyadic trade flows. On the other hand, a GNP-based measure may reflect a growing pie, where increased interdependence with one partner need not lead to a decline in dependence on other partners.

Clearly, we could think of interdependence in both ways. It is inappropriate to say that one is wrong and the other right, since each captures important pieces of information. Therefore I employ two groups of measures of interdependence. One set is constructed using total trade as a control for dyadic flows, and the other uses GDP as the control; I refer to these sets of measures as partner-dependence and economy-dependence measures respectively (Barbieri 1995). There are instances in which one set of measures may be more appropriate than the other, but when speaking about interdependence, in general, both pieces of information contribute to our understanding of this multifaceted phenomenon. Employing alternative measures of interdependence may provide important information about the variations that arise when dependence originates from different sets of factors (e.g., the importance of trade ties for an economy, rather than the relative importance of a given trade partner).

Certainly, dependence, and by extension interdependence, can be thought of as either the relative importance of a particular trading relationship to that which exists with other partners or to the importance of that trading relationship to the overall economy. However, there are practical constraints to relying on GDP-based measures that might make these measures less ideal than others for a given research purpose. For example, data for GNP or GDP are available for only a small number of states in the pre–World War II period. In addition, historical data on total trade tend to be more accurate than data on GNP or GDP, since national trade statistics were recorded for most countries in the nineteenth and earlier twentieth centuries, while the data used to calculate GDP were not systematically compiled by the majority of countries until after 1950. Even then, scholars question the accuracy of these statistics for developing countries, which leads to one of many sources of bias in accurately capturing the third world experience. One characteristic of developing states is that a large percentage of economic activities take place outside the formal sector; that is even true today, but was much more the case prior to World War II. In general, scholars wishing to rely on GDP-based measures restrict the focus of their analysis and the accuracy of those measures for different classes of states. Scholars have made efforts to estimate GDP figures for the pre–World War II era and to adjust post–World War II estimates to account for some of the criticisms of these measures. Still, these estimates are far less reliable than those of recorded economic activities.

Although GDP- or total trade–based measures are the most commonly used means of assessing trade dependence, researchers have proposed a number of alternatives. For example, Polachek (1980) measures the absolute value of dyadic trade flows in his early studies of the trade-conflict relationship, but he also includes GDP as a separate variable among his controls for national attributes. Polachek and McDonald (1992) emphasize the importance of using elasticity of supply and demand to measure the importance of trade flows and to capture a more realistic measure of gains from trade. Similarly, Blanchard and Ripsman (1994) develop a measure of dependence based on the strategic importance of commodities traded with a particular partner. Researchers make a valid point in stressing the need to consider the importance of commodities traded in evaluating trade dependence. However, practical constraints make it difficult to implement their recommendation on a general basis. Unfortunately, the elasticity measures and the measures of the strategic importance of commodities traded require information that is not available for a large number of countries or for a significant period of time. For example, a measure of strategic importance requires information about a state's strategic needs, as well as potential sources of supply and the availability of the commodity. The strategic importance of commodities varies by nation and over time, and data reflecting those variations accurately are difficult to obtain. My goal here is to evaluate a wide range of trading relationships, and this leads me to rely on measures that can be derived for a more general sample of states.

In addition to using different denominators in ratio-level variables, scholars offer a variety of means to combine national-level dependence scores into dyadic-level indices. I find fault with few of the dyadic-level measures employed in trade-conflict literature, with the exception of employing the lower state's dependence score as an indicator of dyadic interdependence (Oneal and Russett 1999). The rationale for this measure is that the least dependent state is the "weakest link," in Dixon's terms (1993); it is less constrained to refrain from force, because it needs the relationship less. Yet, one state does not define a dyadic relationship. Even if one state is less constrained to use force, the state that is more constrained should work harder to resolve a conflict of interest before it escalates. Imagine that State A has two trading partners, State B and State C. State A is not very dependent on either partner, but State B is highly dependent on A, while State C is not. State A's degree of constraint may not vary in these two relationships, but the two partners should vary in their desire and effort to maintain peace in the relationship.

In general, I think it is problematic to employ the characteristics of only one nation when describing the characteristics of a dyad. In fact, I would argue that it contradicts many liberal assumptions about the more open society being able to influence the less open society. For example, U.S. policies based on constructive engagement suggest that Western powers have the capacity and obligation to influence less democratic, economically open states. The weakest link assumption says that China's relationship with the United States should be no different than China's relationship with an autocratic state that has a low level of dependence similar to that of the United States.

Operationalizing Dimensions of Interdependence

In general, the trade-conflict literature emphasizes two dimensions of economic interdependence that I intend to measure: the salience and the symmetry of dependence. By *salience,* I mean the importance of a trading relationship, relative to other trading relationships. Is the level of trade between two states significantly higher than that conducted with other states? Low levels of salience, however equal, may not provide the necessary bonds to deter conflict between states. By *symmetry,* I mean the equality of trade dependence between partners. Are states in a given trading relationship equally dependent upon each other, or is one state much more dependent on the relationship? A large state may rely on a small state for only 10 percent of its total trade, while the small state may depend on the large state for 80 or 90 percent of its imports and exports.

My measure of salience is intended to capture the liberal emphasis on the importance of extensive trade ties, while the symmetry measure captures the concern that some critics have that dependence be balanced. Both elements of interdependence may have an independent effect on trading relationships and also an interactive effect. By interactive effect, I mean that the joint presence of these variables produces more than just the independent additive effect of each variable. Since there may be both an additive and interactive effect from salience and symmetry, I employ a model that incorporates both effects.

For the post–World War II period, I employ two groups of measures of interdependence. One set is constructed using total trade as a control for dyadic flows and the other using GDP as the control.[12] I refer to the measures derived from total trade as *partner-dependence measures,* while those derived from GDP are referred to as *economy-dependence measures.* The partner- and economy-dependence measures are highly correlated, making it difficult to estimate their independent effects simultaneously in a single model. Yet, these measures are conceptually distinct and at times empirically distinct. For example, in the pre–World War II era, the major powers, who have high estimated GDP values, were also the major traders. Therefore, total trade and GDP would be positively correlated. However, in the post–World War II period, there is more variation in the association between GDP and total trade. In general, there is an inverse relationship between a state's dependence on foreign trade, relative to GDP, and the state's level of development (Domke 1988).

It is useful to compare the empirical findings derived from alternative measures of interdependence for two reasons. Measurement choice may affect empirical findings. More important, while alternative measures are often treated as substitutes, I believe they may be capturing different elements of interdependence, whose impact on interstate relations might vary.

First, before building dyadic measures, I construct national measures of dependence for a given relationship. Equation (1) represents *partner dependence*, a measure intended to evaluate the importance of dyadic trade (import and export flows between states composing a dyad) relative to a state's total trade (total exports and imports with all partners),

$$\text{Partner Dependence}_i = \frac{\text{Dyadic Trade}_{ij}}{\text{Total Trade}_i} = \frac{\text{Imports}_{ij} + \text{Exports}_{ij}}{\sum_{k=1}^{N} (\text{Imports}_{ik} + \text{Exports}_{ik})} \quad (1)$$

where N is the number of trade partners for State i. If a state has many trading partners with whom it trades a good deal, then it will not assign much importance to any particular partner. A state's partner-dependence score will be high vis-à-vis another state if the state conducts a large percentage of its trade with that country. Equation (2) contains a measure of *economy dependence*, which is similar in form to partner dependence, but the baseline for evaluating the importance of the dyadic trade flow is the size of the state's economy rather than its total volume of trade:

$$\text{Economy Dependence}_i = \frac{\text{Dyadic Trade}_{ij}}{\text{GDP}_i} = \frac{\text{Imports}_{ij} + \text{Exports}_{ij}}{\text{GDP}_i} . \quad (2)$$

As mentioned, the partner- and economy-dependence measures are highly related to one another (with a correlation of 0.7), but it is possible for them to vary inversely. For example, a state may have high partner dependence and low economy dependence. Such a situation would arise if a state's economy was not heavily dependent upon foreign trade, but the same state elected to conduct most of its trade with a few trade partners. If the state could not acquire certain products domestically and relied on one partner for those products, high partner dependence might reflect a form of dependence not captured with the economy-dependence measure, where the dyadic trade flow would appear minor relative to the national product. On the other hand, if a state was very dependent on foreign trade, relative to national production, but chose to rely on a large number of trading partners, it might have a low partner-dependence score for a relationship, but a high economy-dependence score. In the sample analyzed in this study, the partner-dependence score tends to be higher than the economy-dependence score. Economy dependence was higher than partner dependence in only 8 percent of the observations in the post–World War II period. The economy-dependence measure tends to be higher in cases where states have low GDP values.

After constructing measures of partner dependence and economy dependence for each state in a dyadic relationship, I construct two separate sets of dyadic measures of interdependence. The respective national measures are substituted for the dependence terms in equations (3) and (4) below. The same procedure is used for the total trade– and GDP-based measures.

I require some method of averaging the national dependence scores for each state in a dyad in order to create a dyadic measure of salience. I elected to use the geometric mean, rather than the arithmetic mean, since the former measure assigns a lower value to dyadic salience than the latter when the trade shares for each partner are highly unequal. The presence of one high trade-share will not produce an artificially high measure of dyadic salience, as may be the case if one employs the arithmetic mean for averaging. In addition, the geometric mean will produce scores higher than the arithmetic mean when both states have a high measure of salience, but a score lower than the arithmetic mean when the salience for each state is highly unequal. Salience for a pair of states reflects the extent to which the partners are important to each other; higher dyadic-salience scores indicate that the relationship is important for both partners. The index of dyadic salience is constructed as follows in equation (3):

$$\text{Salience}_{ij} = \sqrt{\text{Dependence}_i \times \text{Dependence}_j}. \qquad (3)$$

While I use the geometric mean in my salience measure to incorporate some consideration of the balance of dependence, I wish to consider the independent effect of symmetry separately. Therefore, I construct an index of symmetry that conforms to a scale similar to that used for the salience score. The index ranges from zero to one, where high values indicate symmetrical ties and low values indicate asymmetrical dependence. When states are equally dependent on the trading relationship, the symmetry score equals one. Simply taking the difference of trade shares would produce a measure where high values would entail asymmetry and low values would denote symmetry. The inverse of this relationship is necessary to provide a scale that conforms to the salience measures.[13] The measure of symmetry is reported in equation (4).

$$Symmetry_{ij} = 1 - |\,Dependence_i - Dependence_j\,| \qquad (4)$$

Clearly, symmetrical ties between states that conduct 10 percent of their trade with each other and between those that conduct 90 percent of their trade with each other constitute different types of relationships. Conceptually, in my view, interdependence involves a combination of salience and symmetry. In other words, a pair of states is highly interdependent, as opposed to dependent or interconnected, only if they trade a lot with each other and their dependence is mutual. This is to say that there is an interaction effect between salience and symmetry, so that the impact of salience on conflict depends on the degree of symmetry in the relationship and vice versa.

Generally, researchers measure the interaction effect of two variables by taking the product of the variables. However, I wish to construct an index of interdependence that is consistent with my theoretical conception of the phenomenon, where salience and symmetry are each important in assessing the level of interdependence in the relationship. Relying on the direct product of salience and symmetry poses theoretical and statistical problems for index construction, since the distribution of the salience measure for my sample has much greater variance than the symmetry measure. With the direct product formulation of the interaction term, salience has a disproportionate influence on the variance in the interdependence index. This formulation also produces an index of interdependence that is highly correlated with the salience variable, creating problems of multicollinearity.

To allow each component of interdependence to contribute equal proportions to an interdependence index, I standardize salience and symmetry by creating z-scores for each variable. There is an important theoretical reason to standardize the variables that create the interaction term. These variables should logically contribute equally to the creation of the interaction. Yet, the distribution of values for these two variables varies considerably, despite the fact that both are measured on a scale ranging from zero to one. This means that the variable salience, which possesses greater variation in its distribution of values, contributes disproportionately to the interaction value. To avoid this result, I have standardized the terms to make sure that both variables have the opportunity to contribute equally to this new variable. Taking the value of each observation, subtracting the mean value of the variable, and dividing that value by its standard deviation creates the z-scores. Standardizing the variables in this fashion reduces the variation in observed values. I then create an interdependence index that is the product of the z-scores of salience and symmetry. This index is reflected in equation (5).

$$\text{Interdependence}_{ij} = \text{Salience}_{ij} \times \text{Symmetry}_{ij} \qquad (5)$$

Standardizing salience and symmetry before constructing the index is also desirable, since it reduces the collinearity between the interaction term and its constituent elements. It is common for an interaction term to be highly collinear with one or more of the variables used to index the interaction effect. However, researchers disagree about whether the additive and interaction effects of variables should be included in a model when variables are highly collinear. In general, researchers disagree over how to handle the problem of high multicollinearity among variables. When variables are highly related, it is difficult to estimate the independent effects of separate variables on the dependent variable (Kennedy 1998, chap. 11). However, Friedrich (1982) demonstrates that it is more desirable to include, rather than exclude, a multiplicative interaction term with the constituent elements used to create it, even if the variables are highly collinear. Unfortunately, many researchers are either unfamiliar with his arguments or view them with skepticism, and consider any estimation derived from models containing highly related variables to be suspect.[14] For this reason, I chose to address the concern of those scholars who argue that multicollinear terms are inappropriate within the context of my interdependence variables, by offering an alternative index to capture the joint effect of salience and symmetry.

For both the partner- and economy-dependence sets of measures, the nonstandardized variables salience and symmetry did not pose problems of multicollinearity. The correlation between these variables was −0.58 and −0.49 for the partner- and economy-dependence measures respectively. The symmetry variable was not highly collinear with a direct-product interaction term (i.e., the interdependence index) for either set of measures. The correlation between symmetry and the nonstandardized interdependence index was −0.45 for the partner-dependence measures and −0.34 for the economy-dependence measures. However, salience and the direct-product interaction term were highly collinear. In the case of the partner-dependence measures, the correlation was 0.96; for the economy-dependence measures, the correlation between salience and the interaction term was 0.94. Creating the standardized index of interdependence reduced the collinearity problem. For the partner-dependence measures, the correlation between salience and the adjusted interdependence index is −0.71, and the correlation between symmetry and the index is 0.63. For the economy-dependence measures, the correlation between salience and the interdependence index is −0.48, and between symmetry and the index is 0.53. Thus, this standardized interdependence index is desirable on theoretical and statistical grounds. It provides an index in which salience and symmetry are equally weighted, and it reduces the problems posed by high collinearity.

Control Variables

In estimating the impact of interdependence on dyadic conflict, it is important to control for factors that might affect both trade and conflict. Otherwise, the relationship between trade and conflict revealed in the analyses may be spurious. The factors that are most germane to my analyses are contiguity, joint democracy, alliance ties, and relative capabilities. The literature suggests that each is theoretically interesting in its own right (Bremer 1992b), but here I am interested in these factors' impact on the trade-conflict relationship.

Contiguity

Empirical tests have consistently revealed that contiguous dyads have both higher levels of trade (Aitken 1973; Arad and Hirsch 1981)[15] and higher levels of conflict (Bremer 1992b; Gochman 1992; Goertz and Diehl 1992; Vasquez 1993).[16] Similarities exist between the arguments advanced to describe the relationship between geography and conflict and those used to explain the impact of economic interdependence. For example, a widely held argument that links geographic proximity to higher levels of conflict is the notion that conflicts of interest are more likely to occur between states that have high levels of contact (Waltz 1979). Goertz and Diehl (1992) explain that borders may create either the context or the issue of a dispute. States may engage in conflict over territorial issues, or their close proximity might give them more interaction opportunities to engage in conflict over other issues (see Vasquez 1993). The same might be said of trade ties—tensions might erupt over trade matters, or the increased interaction associated with trade might lead to conflicts over other issues.

I use the COW contiguity data set[17] to create a dichotomous index of contiguity (by land and by sea up to 400 miles).[18]

Joint Democracy

Controlling for the presence of joint democracy is not only important for its presumed pacifying influence on conflict (see Bremer 1992a, 1992b, 1993; Dixon 1993, 1994; Maoz and Abdolali 1989; Maoz and Russett 1993; Morgan and Campbell 1991; Morgan and Schwebach 1992; Ray 1995; Raymond 1994, 1995; Russett 1993),[19] but also because regime type, political orientation, and other interstate similarities are thought to influence trade relations (Dixon and Moon 1993; Polachek 1997; Pollins 1989a, 1989b).

Additionally, it is important to control for the influence of joint democracy since a high correlation is often assumed to exist between economic (free-market) and political (democratic) freedoms.[20] Dixon (1994) notes the difficulty in disentangling the various normative and structural factors believed to be associated with peace between democratic states. Cultural norms might influence the types of institutional arrangements existing in a nation, while institutions might also affect norms of behavior. It is difficult to determine the causal influence in the relationship between normative and institutional arguments. The problem of mutual influences is compounded when we introduce trade into the equation, since regime type, cultural similarities, and trade patterns have reinforcing influences.

For example, democratic states are less likely to fight each other. We also know that states with similar regime types are more likely to trade

(Dixon and Moon 1993). Polachek (1997) finds that democratic states are more likely to trade with other democratic states and attributes the democratic peace to their high trade ties. Again, the direction of the causal influence is unclear. Regime type can affect trade patterns, but trade patterns might also affect regime type. The expansion of trade ties between states is assumed to give rise to greater commonalties in the social, political, and economic domain. As mentioned earlier, a popular argument advanced in contemporary politics by Western states, such as the case of the United States' trade policy with China, is that trading with an undemocratic state will expose that state to democratic principles and will serve as an impetus for their eventual transition to a more democratic form of government.

Some argue that states with cultural similarities are more likely to trade with each other (Russett 1967). The expansion of trade is also believed to contribute to a convergence of cultures. Thus, culture can affect trade patterns, which in turn can affect cultural similarities. The problem of distinguishing causal influence is compounded when I consider the fact that culture may determine, in part, regime orientation. There may be an interaction effect among these closely related influences. For example, research by Dixon (1994) and Raymond (1994) reveals that democratic states are more likely to pursue nonmilitary and mediated strategies of conflict resolution. The same might be said of trading states. These states should not only have an added incentive to resolve conflicts nonviolently, but should also be better equipped to do so if both states are democratic. Thus, the joint presence of trade ties and democratic institutions may produce different effects than if one of these variables was present alone.

While exploring the connections between regime type and trade is interesting, it is important to remember that the trade-promotes-peace argument is not contingent upon regime type. On the contrary, liberals and other supporters of free trade portray commerce as a means to overcome regime, cultural, and other national divisions. Gasiorowski and Polachek (1982) illustrate this point in their assertion that the increase in trade between the United States and the Eastern bloc nations led to a warming of political relations in the midst of the Cold War. Similarly, Peres and Naor (1993) maintain that the expansion of trade ties among Middle Eastern states will ensure a stable peace in the region.

Data from *Polity III* (Gurr, Jaggers, and Moore 1989; Jaggers and

Gurr 1995, 1996) are used to construct measures of joint democracy. First, I construct national measures of the democratic nature of the regime, using the ordinal measures for institutional democracy and institutional autocracy from *Polity III*. For each state I calculate the value of the democracy score minus the autocracy plus a value of ten, divided by two to average the scores.[21] The two national scores are then combined into a dyadic score (which is the product of the two adjusted democracy scores) designed to capture the interaction effect of joint democracy. The joint democracy measure ranges in value from zero to one hundred and is constructed as follows:

Joint Democracy

$$= \left(\frac{(\text{DemocracyA} - \text{AutocracyA}) + 10}{2} \right) \left(\frac{(\text{DemocracyB} - \text{AutocracyB}) + 10}{2} \right)$$

Alliances

Extensive economic interdependence may be regarded as a form of implicit (economic) alliance; yet, other forms of alliances (formal security alliances) can alter the conflict-proneness of dyadic relationships. Similarly, alliance ties can affect trade patterns. Gowa (1994) shows that states are more likely to trade with their allies during the post–World War II period.[22]

I include a dichotomous index of alliances. Pairs of states with mutual defense pacts, neutrality agreements, or ententes are labeled as allies, receiving a value of one, while dyads without alliances are coded a value of zero.[23] Data are derived from the COW formal alliance data set (Small and Singer 1969).[24]

Relative Power (Capabilities)

The impact of relative power on conflict has received considerable attention, with theorists differing over whether power preponderance or a balance of power is most conducive to promoting peace (Morgenthau 1948; Organski and Kugler 1980; Weede 1976). Recent empirical research at the dyadic level reveals that a preponderance of power is associated with the most peaceful relations (Bremer 1993; Geller 1993). Relative power is important to incorporate in the present analyses, since it may affect both conflict and trade. For example, asymmetrical dependence may reflect other forms of unequal power between states. Dependency theorists and neo-Marxists argue that power shapes economic relationships, resulting in dependence for less powerful states. Liberal economists might also view dependence as being higher between states with unequal power, as a natural result of the heterogeneous factor endowments of developed and developing states, which should lead to greater trade. Interestingly, developed states tend to invest more and trade more with other developed states, despite the similarity of their factor endowments.

I operationalize power using the COW *Composite Index of National Capabilities* (CINC) data set. These data allow me to measure each state's share of the interstate system's total military, industrial, and demographic resources (Bremer 1980, 1992b). The ratio of the larger to smaller state's capabilities is initially calculated. Since this measure is greatly skewed with some very high values present, in the analyses that follow, the log of the larger-smaller ratio is used instead. Theoretically speaking, the log transformation is also a sounder measure, since it implies a decreasing marginal advantage of increasing power differences. For example, it makes little difference whether a state has 100 or 1,000 times more power than its opponent does, since the preponderance of power should produce similar effects when power differences are great.

Temporal Dependence

Logistic regression is used to estimate the impact of interdependence on the probability that a dyad will engage in a dispute.[25] As with ordinary least squares models, logit models assume independence of events, an assumption that is likely violated when analyzing disputes, since the occurrence of one dispute might affect the outbreak of another one. More problematic for an analysis of interstate conflict is the fact that disputes are relatively rare events, and most observations for the dependent variable are zero (nonevents or peace). These nonevents may be related. For example, dyads with long periods of peace are more likely to remain in a peaceful condition and less likely to experience a militarized dispute.

Beck, Katz, and Tucker (1998) recommend a technique to address temporal dependence in logit models with discrete dependent variables, which is now being widely employed in conflict studies. The technique entails including a variable, named peace-years, reflecting the number of years that a particular dyad has remained at peace and a set of cubic splines derived from the peace-years variable. The peace-years variable should be negatively related to dispute occurrence according to the logic that the larger number of years that states in a dyad remain at peace, the less likely they will be to engage in a militarized dispute. In the analyses that follow, Beck, Katz, and Tucker's technique is employed.

EMPIRICAL ANALYSIS

Partner Dependence

Table 2 reports the results of a set of analyses executed with the partner-based dependence measures. The coefficients for the variables salience (β = 7.349), symmetry (β = −2.340), and interdependence (β = 0.045) are all statistically significant. This suggests that it is important to consider several dimensions of interdependence when evaluating trade's impact on conflict. The positive coefficient for salience reveals that dyads with extensive trade ties are more likely than other dyads to engage in conflict. This relationship undercuts the liberal argument that greater trade ties are likely to foster peace. The negative coefficient for symmetry reveals that balanced dependence appears to diminish the conflictual nature of trade ties. Yet, the interdependence index, which assesses the joint effect of salience and symmetry, reveals that a growth in interdependence is positively associated with conflict.

In evaluating the meaning of the coefficients for the additive effects of salience and symmetry versus the joint effect represented by the interdependence index, it is useful to interpret the respective coefficients of salience and symmetry when one condition is set equal to zero. For example, imagine a case in which a dyad is highly asymmetrical, with the value of symmetry being zero. Under these conditions, only the salience coefficient would be relevant for assessing the impact of trade ties on conflict. Symmetry and the interdependence index would be equal to zero, so they would have no impact on the estimated effects on conflict. Thus, the coefficient for salience provides the estimated impact of this variable when symmetry is equal to zero, while the coefficient for symmetry provides the estimate of its impact when salience is equal to zero. The latter situation would not be substantively interesting in terms of assessing the impact of symmetry, since zero salience means zero trade. The fact that dependence is perfectly symmetrical simply means that the states composing the dyad are completely equal in their absence of dependence. Of more substantive relevance is the question of how the expansion of trade ties might have a differing effect at various levels of symmetry. By estimating the joint effect of salience and symmetry with the interdependence index, I am assuming that the individual contribution of either salience or symmetry to dyadic conflict, expressed in their respective coefficients, may vary across different ranges of the other variable. For example, the impact of salience may vary across different ranges of values for symmetry—trade dependence may have a different effect when sym-

TABLE 2. INTERDEPENDENCE AND
DISPUTES, 1870–1992 (USING PARTNER-
DEPENDENCE MEASURES)

Independent Variables	Dispute Occurrence$_t$
Salience$_{t-1}$	7.349***
	(0.924)
Symmetry$_{t-1}$	−2.340***
	(0.438)
Interdependence$_{t-1}$	0.045***
	(0.011)
Contiguity$_{t-1}$	1.892***
	(0.079)
Joint democracy$_{t-1}$	−0.012***
	(0.001)
Alliance$_{t-1}$	0.145*
	(0.076)
Relative capabilities$_{t-1}$	−0.088***
	(0.023)
Peace	−0.361***
	(0.019)
Spline 1	−0.002***
	(0.000)
Spline 2	0.001***
	(0.000)
Spline 3	0.000
	(0.000)
Constant	−0.725
	(0.468)
χ^2	4,024.74***
Log-likelihood	−5,091.75
Pseudo R^2	0.26
N	138,065

Note: Robust standard errors appear in parentheses.
Significance levels refer to two-tailed tests.
*$p \leq .05$, **$p \leq .01$, ***$p \leq .001$

metry is low and high. Likewise, symmetry may have a differing effect when salience is low, compared to when it is high.

The statistically significant sign for the interdependence index reveals that there is an interaction effect present. Given the nonlinear nature of logit estimates, it is easier to evaluate the overall relationship of interdependence and conflict through graphical means. I use the estimated coefficients from the logit analysis to evaluate the impact on conflict at various combinations of trade dependence. In figure 2, I graph the possible values of salience, symmetry, and the interdependence index. The horizontal axis represents the share of each state's trade with its partner. These trade shares are used in conjunction with the logit estimates to produce a surface plane that corresponds to the probability of conflict present at the various combinations of trade shares. The figure demonstrates that at the lower levels of interdependence, trade does not appear to have a dramatic impact on conflict. There is some evidence that asymmetrical ties are more conflictual than symmetrical ties at the low range of trade dependence. As mentioned previously, this corresponds to the negative coefficient for symmetry when salience is set equal to zero. Once dependence grows for each partner, the likelihood that a dyad will experience a dispute increases, as revealed by the positive coefficients for salience and the interdependence index. Dyads with both extensive and symmetrical ties appear to be the most conflictual. Mutual dependence might diminish conflict at lower levels of dependence, but at higher levels of dependence, the effect is reversed. The evidence contradicts the assumption that high interdependence promotes peace. It also shows that there are variations in the impact of interdependence at different levels of salience. The findings suggests that mutual dependence may diminish conflict, but only when dependence is limited.

Fortunately, most states depend very little on any single trade partner. Thus, most dyads fall within the lower ranges of values observed on the surface plane, where conflict is less likely. Moreover, dependence tends to be balanced. Yet, the balance occurs because each state in a dyadic relationship depends very little on its partner. It is balanced because most states are relatively equal in their tendency to keep dependence low.

The control variables yield few surprises for those familiar with empirical studies of dyadic conflict. The positive coefficient for contiguity indicates that contiguous dyads are more conflictual than noncontiguous dyads. Dyads that are jointly democratic are less conflictual than others,

THE LIBERAL ILLUSION

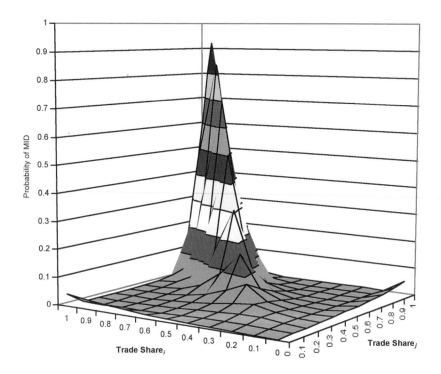

FIG. 2. Partner dependence and dispute probabilities

as indicated by the negative coefficient for this variable. The bonds represented by alliances, like those of trade, do not appear to reduce the likelihood of conflict; instead alliances tend to be positively associated with conflict. Once again, this raises questions about the view that bonds between states foster peace. The coefficient for relative power reveals that dyads with unequal power are more peaceful. The peace counter is negative and statistically significant, as expected, suggesting that those dyads with a longer history of peace are less likely to experience a dispute. The coefficients for the spline variables indicate that the temporal dependence between observations diminishes as time (i.e., peace-years) increases.

In considering the empirical findings for the components of interdependence, it appears that the extensiveness of trade ties has the greatest influence on the probability of conflict. This raises the question of whether the explanatory power of the estimated model might be improved if we considered only the salience of the economic relationship. Do symmetry and the interaction effect captured by the interdependence index improve our understanding of dyadic conflict, or is it sufficient to consider simply the extent of the trade ties? To answer this question, I compared alternative model specifications to determine whether including particular variables improves the explanatory power of the model. I do this by using a likelihood ratio test to assess whether excluding a variable significantly weakens the explanatory power of the model.

First, the full model reported in table 2 is estimated. Then it is compared to a model excluding each of the components of interdependence in turn. If excluding a variable does not reduce the power of the model, then the variable may not provide sufficient enhancement to the model to warrant its inclusion. I first exclude the interdependence index to determine whether the additive model of salience and symmetry provides similar results to those obtained with the fuller model. When the likelihood ratio test reveals a statistically significant chi-square value, it means that the saturated model is preferred to the restricted model, the one that excludes the added variable of interest. When I exclude the interdependence index from the estimated model, salience and symmetry remain statistically significant, and the directional influence of their coefficients is similar to that reported in table 2. The magnitude of the coefficients for salience increases to 9.40, while the magnitude of the coefficient for the variable symmetry declines to −0.59.

The likelihood ratio test reveals that the model including the interaction effect captured in the interdependence index is better than the model excluding it, at the 0.00001 level of significance. Next, I excluded the symmetry variable from the full model and found that its exclusion also reduced the explanatory power of the model. The likelihood ratio test was significant at the 0.00001 level. Once again, the directional influence for the remaining variables, salience and the interdependence index, remains similar to that observed in the saturated model. The magnitude of the influence for salience is greater (with a coefficient of 16.81), while that for symmetry is reduced to −0.78. The saturated model is also significantly better than the model containing salience alone with the control variables.

There are, of course, many criteria for evaluating whether to include a variable in a statistical model, only one of which is its contribution to the explanatory power of the model. Including variables for theoretical reasons may be viewed as equally important. In this case, including the separate components of interdependence and assessing their additive and interactive effects are deemed desirable on statistical and theoretical grounds. Thus, in the remainder of this study, I rely on models that account for the independent and joint contribution of salience and symmetry.

We might also consider whether including economic relationships at all improves our understanding of conflict beyond that obtained by simply including the control variables. The control variables reflect the more traditional concerns of conflict theorists who have, until recently, largely ignored the role of economic relationships in studies of interstate conflict. A comparison of models containing and excluding the economic variables examined here reveals that their inclusion significantly improves the explanatory power of the model. Economic ties do matter for understanding interstate conflict, but they matter in ways that are unanticipated by liberals.

Economy Dependence

Next, I consider whether the results obtained with the partner-dependence measures are similar to those obtained when employing the economy-dependence measures. Table 3 reports the results of analyses that employ the latter measures. Recall that the economy-dependence measure differs from the partner-dependence measure in that the latter measure weights the importance of trade flows relative to GDP, rather than total trade. Unfortunately, researchers wishing to evaluate the importance of a given trade flow relative to a nation's GDP must confine their analysis to the post–World War II period, unless they wish to rely upon a very limited sample of cases. This approach, in turn, leads to qualifications about the trade-conflict relationship. It is still useful to compare the findings from these measures with those obtained from the partner-based measures of interdependence to determine whether the findings remain robust across measures and whether there may be real differences in the consequences of different forms of dependence.

The results reported in table 3 are similar to those that I report in table 2 above. Specifically, the coefficients for salience ($\beta = 11.111$), symmetry ($\beta = -4.235$), and the interdependence index ($\beta = 0.028$) are all statistically significant and reveal a pattern consistent with that reported in the analysis of the partner-based measures of interdependence. In this case, the choice of measurement does not appear to alter my empirical findings. Whether I employ total trade or GDP-based measures of interdependence, the consequences appear similar. Interdependence fails to inhibit conflict. Instead, high interdependence appears to be associated with more conflictual relations than low dependence.

The control variables also reveal patterns similar to those found in the previous analysis, with the exception of the alliance variable. Here, the

TABLE 3. INTERDEPENDENCE AND
DISPUTES, 1948-92 (USING ECONOMY-
DEPENDENCE MEASURES)

Independent Variables	Dispute Occurrence$_t$
Salience$_{t-1}$	11.111***
	(3.416)
Symmetry$_{t-1}$	−4.235***
	(0.969)
Interdependence$_{t-1}$	0.028**
	(0.011)
Contiguity$_{t-1}$	2.022***
	(0.088)
Joint Democracy$_{t-1}$	−0.011***
	(0.001)
Alliance$_{t-1}$	0.123
	(0.092)
Relative capabilities$_{t-1}$	−0.081**
	(0.027)
Peace	−0.419***
	(0.024)
Spline 1	−0.002***
	(0.000)
Spline 2	0.001***
	(0.000)
Spline 3	0.000
	(0.000)
Constant	−1.353
	(0.999)
χ^2	2,922.92***
Log-likelihood	−3,449.62
Pseudo R^2	0.28
N	119,296

Note: Robust standard errors appear in parentheses.
Significance levels refer to two-tailed tests.
*$p \leq .05$, **$p \leq .01$, ***$p \leq .001$

alliance coefficient is positive, as in the first analysis, but it lacks statistical significance. Since the two analyses are conducted on different historical periods, one might conclude that the findings result from historical differences in the relationship between alliances and conflict. To determine whether this is the case, I examined the bivariate effect of alliance ties on interstate conflict in the pre–World War II and post–World War II samples, in addition to the full sample. In all cases, the bivariate analyses of alliance ties and conflict revealed a statistically significant positive relationship. However, when the logit model reported in table 2 is estimated with the other control variables, the alliance variable remained positive, but lacked statistical significance when samples of the pre–World War II and post–World War II periods were analyzed separately. Thus, we might conclude that the effect of alliance ties is weak when controlling for other factors or that it reveals itself only in large samples, but not smaller ones.

To what extent does the trade-conflict relationship itself vary across historical periods? Since the partner-based measures of interdependence are the only measures that allow me to look at both the pre–World War II and post–World War II period, separate analyses on these two periods are estimated. The results of this comparative analysis are reported in table 4. Although there is some variation in the magnitude of the coefficients, the basic pattern of the trade-conflict relationship appears consistent across time. Variations in interdependence at the system and dyadic level may have occurred over time, as a result of increased globalization, but trade's impact on conflict does not appear to have changed.

In sum, the empirical findings fail to offer support for the liberal argument that trade promotes peace. At the same time, the empirical analyses fail to offer overwhelming support for the critical view that symmetrical ties may be more beneficial. Symmetrical relations appear to be less conflictual when trade ties are minor, but the pacifying influence of mutual dependence is not observed at high levels of dependence. This suggests that the extensiveness of trade ties are the dominant factor in evaluating the impact of trade on conflict. Moreover, the argument that trade ties are unimportant relative to more traditional factors believed to influence conflict lacks empirical support. Including economic interdependence in our analyses of conflict improves the predictive power of our models.

An optimistic reading of the findings presented here would be that few states rely heavily on other states. Therefore, most dyads experience very limited interdependence, and so they fall within the lower range of values observed in my illustrations. It is here that symmetrical ties may offer some hope for reducing the conflict propensity of dyadic relationships. Unfortunately, the findings suggest that efforts to expand trade ties in the hopes of producing extensive interdependence may result in less peaceful relationships. The wisest strategy for a leader to adopt appears to be

TABLE 4. INTERDEPENDENCE AND DISPUTES, COMPARING HISTORICAL PERIODS (USING PARTNER-DEPENDENCE MEASURES)

Independent Variables	Dispute Occurrence$_t$	
	1870–1944	1945–92
Salience$_{t-1}$	6.449***	8.723***
	(1.533)	(1.420)
Symmetry$_{t-1}$	−2.939***	−2.264***
	(0.856)	(0.497)
Interdependence$_{t-1}$	0.057**	0.042***
	(0.022)	(0.011)
Contiguity$_{t-1}$	1.284***	1.976***
	(0.147)	(0.090)
Joint Democracy$_{t-1}$	−0.014***	−0.012***
	(0.002)	(0.001)
Alliance$_{t-1}$	0.212	0.093
	(0.174)	(0.090)
Relative capabilities$_{t-1}$	−0.144**	−0.080**
	(0.047)	(0.027)
Peace	−0.257***	−0.410***
	(0.035)	(0.024)
Spline 1	−0.001***	−0.002***
	(0.000)	(0.000)
Spline 2	0.001**	0.001***
	(0.000)	(0.000)
Spline 3	−0.000	−0.000
	(0.000)	(0.000)
Constant	0.125	−0.692
	(0.893)	(0.533)
χ^2	593.51***	3,030.18***
Log-likelihood	−1,493.88	−3,534.04
Pseudo R^2	0.17	0.29
N	16,783	121,282

Note: Robust standard errors appear in parentheses. Significance levels refer to two-tailed tests.
*$p \le .05$, **$p \le .01$, ***$p \le .001$

restricting the extent to which he or she allows his or her state to become dependent upon any other state or on the global economy as a whole. Limited dependence may offer states the ability to reap the benefits of trade, without subjecting themselves to the costly aspects of interdependence, such as the threats to national autonomy that may result in tension.

In addition to contradicting conventional liberal wisdom, the empirical findings are inconsistent with some published evidence that supports the view that trade promotes peace (e.g., Oneal et al. 1996; Oneal and Ray 1997; Oneal and Russett 1997). The differences in empirical findings across studies might be attributable to a number of factors. First, most alternative studies focus on a more limited domain of cases than that explored here, such as "politically relevant dyads." However, the relationships that I report in this chapter apply to "politically relevant" and "non-relevant" dyads (Barbieri 1998). Some might assume that the differences in findings might result from alternative measurements of interdependence. The findings presented here do not reveal significant differences across results obtained with total trade– and GDP-based measures, but measurement choice may prove to be one source of variation in empirical findings if additional measures were compared. The more likely explanation is that relying on different measures means including different cases in one's analysis, since data may be missing for some variables and not others. In addition, researchers differ in the manner in which they measure conflict. Even studies that focus on MIDs code the dependent variable differently. Some scholars code multiple-year disputes as one for every year in which the dispute is ongoing. Finally, researchers employ different control variables. Even when using the same control variables, researchers differ on how they measure them. The potential sources of variation have been explored elsewhere (Barbieri 1996c, 1998), but no conclusive evidence indicates the source of the variation in findings.

This leads to the question of why researchers reach different conclusions about the trade-conflict relationship. Differences arising from sample or measurement variation would suggest that trade's impact is not consistent across all types of relationships or that different forms of dependence captured by alternative measures may have alternative consequences for interstate relations. The variations in empirical findings might not be a simple statistical artifact, but may reflect real differences in trade's impact. This, in itself, is important to consider. It suggests that the results found here only scratch the surface of the more significant question of why variations obtain in trading relationships. When taken as a whole, what should be obvious from the trade-conflict literature is the absence of firm evidence that trade promotes peace. If such evidence existed, I would expect this relationship to remain robust across studies.

Does this mean that the liberal vision of trade's pacifying effect is unwarranted? Not necessarily—trade may improve the ability of states to resolve the most serious conflicts and to prevent them from escalating into the deadliest types of battles. Recall that militarized interstate disputes may include threats, displays, or uses of force. Even among events in which force is used, there are variations in the intensities of conflicts. In the next chapter, I investigate whether interdependent states experience different types of military conflicts than do other dyads.

Chapter 4

INTERDEPENDENCE,
NEGOTIATION, AND ESCALATION

The empirical evidence presented in chapter 3 suggests that interdependent dyads are more likely than others to engage in militarized disputes. Does this mean that liberal assumptions about trade's pacifying and unifying power are completely unfounded? We know that trade ties fail to prevent the outbreak of militarized conflicts, but the question remains whether the conflicts that arise between interdependent states are less severe than those found in relationships where the bonds created by trade ties are absent. This question has drawn little attention, since the focus of previous work has been on trade's impact on the *occurrence* of conflict. However, there are good reasons to expect that interdependence might affect other stages of the conflict process. Interdependence may have an impact on the resolution or the escalation of conflict that is different from its impact on the occurrence of conflict. In this chapter, I explore the impact that interdependence has on the characteristics of dyadic conflict.

THEORETICAL BACKGROUND

The logic of liberalism may be extended to the evolution of disputes. Both the economic incentives to refrain from conflict and the positive sociological bonds between trading partners that liberals attribute to trade should also have an effect beyond the outbreak of conflict. Vuchinich and Teachman (1993) present a framework for evaluating the utility of conflict beyond its initiation stage; their framework is useful to consider within the context of interdependent relationships. They argue that as a conflict unfolds, leaders persist in assessing the utility of continuing the conflict and bring it to an end when costs outweigh benefits. Polachek's (1980) expected-utility model of the trade-conflict relationship can also be extended to dispute evolution. As discussed previously, Polachek argues that leaders are deterred from initiating conflict against important trading partners for fear of losing the welfare gains associated with trade. Considering the evidence presented in chapter 3, one might conclude that the anticipation of losses does not create a sufficient deterrent to conflict initiation. Yet, the actual realization of these trade-related losses may prove to have a strong influence on decisions to terminate conflicts rapidly and to prevent them from escalating. Thus, among the costs of continuing a conflict, a leader might consider the mounting economic hardships associated with harming an important trading relationship and thus be motivated to bring the conflict to an end. Barbieri and Bremer (1998) provide evidence that dyads with high levels of trade experience shorter disputes than dyads with less extensive trade ties.

In addition to the economic incentives hypothesized to motivate leaders to terminate conflicts before they escalate, liberals suggest that interdependent actors have an enhanced ability to settle conflicts nonviolently and that extensive linkages (including but not limited to trade) facilitate the creation of mechanisms conducive for achieving the peaceful resolution of conflicts. This should prevent interdependent states from engaging in any form of conflict. Yet, we know that such conflicts occur. Still, if liberal predictions about trade's pacifying power are at all correct, I would expect that at a minimum interdependent dyads should be better able than other dyads to negotiate a settlement to conflicts that break out and to prevent them from escalating. Disputes among interdependent dyads should be less intense than those experienced in other relationships.

The question remains, are conflicts between interdependent dyads really less intense than those found in other relationships? Psychological and sociological theories offer conflicting interpretations about the nature of conflict in interdependent relationships. The expansion of social bonds may at times facilitate conflict resolution (Rubin, Pruitt, and Kim 1994). On the other hand, there is evidence that when conflicts do arise between interdependent actors they may be more intense than those found in other relationships. In thinking about why this might be the case, we can consider alternative forms of relationships in which actors have much in common, experience high levels of interaction, and are intimately connected by a web of linkages. As discussed earlier, civil wars and family and marital violence illuminate the potential for intense conflict in interdependent relations. While primarily concerned with interpersonal relations, the expanding interdisciplinary research on close relationships identifies the dynamics of such relations and the potential for actors who are intimately connected to experience intense conflict (Bercheid et al. 1989; Hendrick 1989). This literature is useful to consider within the context of interdependent relationships between states.

Many of the theories concerning close relationships have their roots in the work of Freud (1938, 370; 1948, 54, 55), and his conception of ambivalence in intimate relations (Coser 1956, 61–62, esp. fn. 60–62). Freud argues that within close relationships it is natural for an individual to develop hostility toward those individuals with whom he or she is intimately involved, such as family members or marital relations. In the interest of preserving peace in close relationships, individuals have a tendency to suppress their hostilities. However, feelings of love and hate may be commingled in intimate relations. When conflicts do erupt within intimate relations, they are more likely to be more intense in nature than conflicts found between actors with limited bonds. The issue serving as the catalyst for any particular conflict may have little surface connection to the overall source of tension in a given relationship. Still, in close relationships the conflict that results may incorporate the hostile feelings originating from other issues. If we apply this dynamic to interstate relations, one might argue that important trade partners should suppress their hostilities about issues such as the distribution of gains from trade. Yet, if a conflict does erupt over trade or other issues, pent-up hostilities may be unleashed, leading to more violent confrontations than would exist in a conflict between less interdependent states.

Interdependent relations tend to exhibit the competing forces of cooperation and conflict, analogous to the love-hate relationships described by Freud and others. Simmel's (1955) and Coser's (1956) assessments of interpersonal and intergroup relations provide clues about why conflicts that erupt among interdependent states might be more intense than those conflicts found among less interdependent states. In interpersonal relationships, the intensity of conflict is directly related to the emotional investment in the relationship. In a similar way, one could argue that the more states become involved and dependent upon each other, the greater potential for hostilities to arise over a host of issues and the more intense those conflicts will be. Coser explains:

> Conflict is more passionate and more radical when it arises out of close relationships. The coexistence of union and opposition in such relations makes for the peculiar sharpness of conflict. Enmity calls forth deeper and more violent reactions, the greater the involvement of the parties among whom it originates. (1956, 71)

The conditions under which hostilities will be suppressed or expressed in interdependent relations remain unclear. Given the economic and sociological motivations to refrain from harming an important trading relationship, we might expect important trading partners to repress tensions that arise in such relationships. This view might lead one to predict that interdependent relationships would witness less frequent conflict than other types of relationships. Coser suggests that the greater the involvement of actors and the more they have invested in a relationship, the more likely they will be to suppress their hostilities (chaps. 3–4). Nevertheless, the outbreak of a conflict could unleash suppressed hostilities and lead to particularly intense disputes. Coser adds that when institutional mechanisms exist to dissipate or channel hostile feelings, actors are more likely to suppress hostilities. Hostilities may even be directed toward a target other than the initial source of tensions. Drawing on liberal theories of interstate linkages, we would expect trade ties to facilitate the types of formal and informal mechanisms that serve to dissipate tensions.

Interdependent states should be motivated to protect the benefits enjoyed in such relationships and to suppress the hostilities that might arise over issues such as the distribution of gains from trade. I would therefore expect interdependent states to seek negotiated settlements to conflicts, rather than resorting to some form of military engagement. Still, the conditions under which hostilities will be suppressed, expressed, or intensified remain unclear. For this reason, I wish to examine whether interdependent states are better able than others to resolve their conflicts through negotiation. Moreover, it is unclear whether the enhanced mechanisms for conflict resolution presumed to exist in interdependent relationships necessarily mean that conflicts within such relationships would be less likely than others not to escalate in severity. Therefore, I also explore that issue here.

RESEARCH STRATEGY

To find out whether interdependence affects the manner in which disputes are settled or escalate, I focus exclusively on cases of disputing dyads—those in which a dyad experiences a militarized interstate dispute, rather than examining all dyadic relationships as in my previous analyses. Once again, I focus on the period 1870–1992 for analyzing the partner-dependence measures of interdependence and the post–World War II period for the economy-dependence measures.

Focusing exclusively on disputing dyads raises the question of whether sampling bias would affect my analysis. For example, if leaders systematically evaluated trade dependence with potential adversaries and refrained from participating in conflicts with important trading partners, then states would "select" into conflicts with other states only when they perceived potential threats to trading relationships to be low. Disputing dyads would therefore reflect this selection process, and the resulting sample would be different from the general population of dyads. It would be difficult to identify any association between trade and conflict escalation, if the existence of trade ties prevented states from entering conflicts.

While concerns about biased sampling may be warranted in studies focusing exclusively on disputing dyads, in the analyses presented here they do not appear to pose a problem. There is no reason to believe that leaders select their disputes based on trade-related factors or that disputing dyads have different types of trading relationships than other dyads. Similarly, we cannot assume that states only engage in conflict when they perceive that trade-related costs would be low. Based on the evidence presented in chapter 3—that interdependent dyads are more likely to experience MIDs—it might be more reasonable to argue that any sample of disputing dyads would contain a disproportionate share of interdependent dyads. Nevertheless, I believe that a state's decision to engage in a conflict arises from a complex series of events and interactions, rather than trade-related considerations alone. Thus, the sample of disputing dyads should be reflective of the general range of trading and interdependent relationships present in a general population of dyads. This means it is possible to assess the impact of interdependence at the dispute stage of the conflict process.

Most disputes (85 percent) involve only two states, and I focus on this sample. Deriving dyadic measures of dispute characteristics is difficult in struggles involving more than two states, since the characteristics describing the conflict may not be applicable to all states participating in the dispute. For example, the MID data set includes a variable for highest level of force employed in a conflict. States may be listed as participating in a dispute, but exit the conflict before it escalates to its highest level of conflict severity. Therefore, if I wish to ascribe the dispute characteristics to all the participants of the conflict, it is necessary to focus on one-on-one conflicts. In multiple-party disputes, states may enter and leave the conflict at different times, and in some cases states on opposite sides of a dispute may not even have any overlapping period of participation. Moreover, Jones, Bremer, and Singer (1996) demonstrate that the joining of disputes by third parties leads to conflicts that are systematically different from those that remain one-on-one in nature (e.g., they are longer in duration). To avoid dealing with the compounding effect of dispute joining in this analysis, I focus exclusively on disputes that begin and remain one-on-one.

Values for the dependent variable correspond to the year of the dispute, while a one-year lag is introduced for the independent variables to preclude reverse causality (see discussion in chap. 3). The control variables employed in the previous chapter are also included, with the exception of the control for temporal dependence. This control is excluded, since the problem of a preponderance of peace-years does not pose a problem for this analysis where the unit of observation is the disputing dyad.

The dispute data set contains information about several characteristics of a dispute, including its settlement type, battle fatalities, and highest level of force employed. Ideally, we would explore the sequential process associated with the unfolding of an event to determine the stages at which interdependence mattered. Unfortunately, data limitations make this approach difficult to pursue. The measures employed offer only a crude indication of dispute escalation. For example, states may choose to employ a high level of force at the onset of a conflict, which would entail no escalation from threats to displays or uses of force. Thus, while the relevant hypotheses are framed in terms of the restraint imposed on conflict escalation by interdependence, I am essentially estimating whether trade ties prevent the most serious disputes from occurring. Although the characteristics of conflict analyzed may appear redundant, multiple measures are included to provide a more comprehensive assessment of the relationship between trade and the conflict process.

I first examine whether interdependent dyads are better able than other dyads to achieve negotiated settlements to conflicts. I then investigate whether conflicts are more severe among more interdependent dyads than among other dyads. The dispute data set contains information about the type of settlement reached in a dispute and includes four categories: negotiated, imposed, none, and unclear. Since I am interested in whether negotiated settlements are achieved, I employ a dichotomous measure of negotiation, where dyads are coded with a value of one if they settle a dispute through negotiation and a value of zero otherwise.

Next, I explore whether more interdependent dyads are less likely than others to engage in the most serious form of dispute behavior, interstate war. Two closely related tests are undertaken. First, I examine whether interdependent dyads are less likely than others to engage in wars, as defined by the COW standard of 1,000 battle fatalities (Small and Singer 1982, 55, 59). A dichotomous measure is employed in which the occurrence of a war is coded a value of one and a nonoccurrence is coded zero in a particular disputing dyad. An additional test of trade's impact on dispute severity is conducted, where severity is measured employing the fatality-level variable from the dispute data set. Fatality level is an ordinal-level variable divided into the following categories based on battle-related fatalities: (1) no fatalities; (2) 1–25 fatalities; (3) 26–100 fatalities; (4) 101–250 fatalities; (5) 251–500 fatalities; (6) 501–999 fatalities; and (7) 1,000 or more fatalities (Jones, Bremer, and Singer 1996).

In preliminary analyses, I also examined whether more interdependent dyads are more likely than others to confine their conflicts to threats, rather than engaging in higher levels of force. The use-of-force variable, also derived from the dispute data set, is an ordinal measure containing four categories of conflict behavior: (1) threat to use force; (2) display of force; (3) the actual use of force; and (4) war. I found no significant relationship between the interdependence measures or any of the control variables and the use-of-force category, and therefore I have decided to forgo reporting these results.

Again, I employ logit regression analysis to estimate the relationship between trade and the two dichotomous dependent variables (negotiated settlement and interstate war). Due to the fact that the fatalities variable is an ordinal categorical dependent variable, I use a specialized form of logit, ordered logit.[1] Ordered logit models permit me to estimate the probability that dyads will fall within a particular category of conflict severity. In addition to estimating the coefficients corresponding to each explanatory variable, the models estimate the threshold parameters separating adjacent categories of dispute intensity and severity. Estimates provide the underlying probability that dyads fall within a particular category, based in part on the explanatory factors included in the model and in part on the unobserved factors influencing the distribution of dyads. The cut points reported for each model refer to the threshold parameters between categories of the ordinal variable.

EMPIRICAL RESULTS

Negotiated Settlements

Table 5 reports the results of the logit analysis estimating the impact of interdependence on the probability of achieving a negotiated settlement to a dispute. The results obtained when employing the partner-based measures of interdependence appear in column 1, while the results for the economy-dependence measures appear in column 2. The analysis with the partner-dependence measures includes the period 1870–1992,

TABLE 5. INTERDEPENDENCE AND NEGOTIATED SETTLEMENTS

	Settlement	
Independent Variables	Partner Dependence	Economy Dependence
Salience$_{t-1}$	8.178**	19.881
	(2.141)	(15.627)
Symmetry$_{t-1}$	0.478	3.392
	(1.030)	(4.198)
Interdependence$_{t-1}$	0.161*	0.132*
	(0.075)	(0.064)
Contiguity$_{t-1}$	0.493*	0.675
	(0.227)	(0.369)
Joint democracy$_{t-1}$	0.007*	0.008
	(0.003)	(0.004)
Alliance$_{t-1}$	−0.022	0.477
	(0.224)	(0.270)
Relative capabilities$_{t-1}$	−0.006	0.172
	(0.077)	(0.095)
Constant	−2.759*	−6.557
	(1.084)	(4.199)
χ^2	25.83***	19.73**
Log-likelihood	−375.62	−221.01
Pseudo R^2	0.03	0.04
N	845	603

Note: Robust standard errors appear in parentheses.
Significance levels refer to two-tailed tests.
*$p \leq .05$, **$p \leq .01$, ***$p \leq .001$

while the analysis with the economy-dependence measures includes the period 1948–92. However, no discernible differences were found in the trade-conflict relationship in separate historical eras. While the former analysis is considered more generalizable since it includes a broader spatial and temporal domain, both measures are included to assess whether differences exist over measurement choice and over these different types of dependence.

The first set of results reveals that salience and interdependence are both statistically significant and positively associated with negotiated settlements to disputes. This finding is consistent with the liberal view that the expansion of trade ties is conducive to conflict resolution. Symmetry does not appear to have an independent effect on achieving negotiated settlements. However, when symmetry is combined with extensive ties, dyads are more likely to obtain such outcomes, as revealed by the interdependence index. It appears that it is the salience of the relationship or the extent of trade ties that is driving the positive relationship between interdependence and negotiated settlements.

The results for the analysis with the economy-dependence measures yield a slightly different picture. In this case, only the joint effect of salience and symmetry, captured in the interdependence index, is statistically significant. Dyads that are both symmetrical and salient appear to be more likely to achieve negotiated settlements. As I noted in the last chapter, the interdependence index captures the high end of the interdependence spectrum, suggesting that the benefits of conflict resolution mechanisms are mainly enjoyed when interdependence is high. There are no theoretical reasons to anticipate differences in the results derived with the two different sets of measures. In general, economy dependence is higher for states with small, rather than large economies. Partner dependence is contingent upon a state's total number of trading partners, which may or may not be related to its economic size. The variations in significance levels in the two analyses reported here may not result from real differences in the types of dependence, but may simply be the product of the smaller sample size in the latter analysis. Taken together, however, the results offer a similar picture. High interdependence does appear to increase the likelihood of achieving a negotiated settlement to conflict.

The coefficients pertaining to the control variables in the first analysis reveal that contiguous dyads and jointly democratic dyads are also more likely to achieve negotiated settlements. Alliance ties and relative power appear to have little effect on settlement outcomes. In the second analysis, contiguity and joint democracy fall short of the minimum 0.05 significance level established for all the analyses in this study. But they approach this threshold with a significance level of 0.06, suggesting that there is likely an empirical connection.

We might conclude that interdependent dyads, because they are better able to negotiate conflict, are less likely to permit them to escalate. Yet, the relationship between negotiation and conflict escalation is not clear-cut. Negotiation might follow the escalation of conflict. In fact, states may have greater incentives to negotiate serious conflicts than less severe ones. Thus, the question remains whether interdependent dyads are less likely to experience serious conflicts. To address this question I turn to an analysis of war and dispute severity.

The Escalation of Disputes to War

One way to determine whether interdependence affects the severity of conflict is to examine whether trade ties affect the probability that dyads will engage in the most serious disputes—wars. Table 6 illustrates the results of logit analyses of interdependence and war, where the results of analysis with the partner-dependence measures are reported in column 1 and those with the economy-dependence measures are reported in column 2. There are some variations across these two analyses. In the case of the partner-dependence measure, I find that salience or the extensiveness of trade ties increases the likelihood that a dyad will experience a war. The symmetrical nature of the ties does not appear to matter, nor does the multiplicative term representing the interaction effect of salience and symmetry. For the economy-dependence measure, the interdependence index is the only statistically significant variable, and it is positively associated with war involvement. In the latter analysis, war appears more likely only in those cases that have high salience and high symmetry, while in the former, war is more likely among salient trading relations, regardless of the degree of balanced dependence. There appear to be differences across the two types of dependence, but in general, the substantive interpretation of the findings is consistent. Trade does not appear to prevent dyads from engaging in the most serious conflicts. In fact, serious conflicts appear to be more likely for highly interdependent states. In the case of partner dependence, extensive ties appear to be associated with escalation to war, regardless of the balance of dependence. With respect to economy dependence, extensive and symmetrical ties are positively associated with wars. The findings are consistent with the view that extensive ties may lead to severe conflicts.

Surprisingly, none of the control variables is statistically significant in either analysis. These variables are generally assumed to be better predictors of war involvement than are economic relationships. Using the likelihood ratio test to determine whether considering these control variables improves my statistical explanation of war, I find that their inclusion does not improve the estimated model significantly. Through a series of tests comparing the explanatory power of alternative models with the likelihood ratio test, I found that models estimating the salience of the economic relationship appear to offer the best fit for explaining war involvement. However, it would be difficult to justify excluding the con-

TABLE 6. INTERDEPENDENCE AND WAR

	War Occurrence$_t$	
Independent Variables	Partner Dependence	Economy Dependence
Salience$_{t-1}$	11.394**	61.156
	(3.985)	(35.395)
Symmetry$_{t-1}$	1.033	6.502
	(1.606)	(8.894)
Interdependence$_{t-1}$	0.253	0.499**
	(0.136)	(0.205)
Contiguity$_{t-1}$	0.389	0.217
	(0.642)	(1.516)
Joint Democracy$_{t-1}$	−0.010	0.015
	(0.013)	(0.015)
Alliance$_{t-1}$	−0.308	−0.038
	(0.579)	(0.855)
Relative capabilities$_{t-1}$	0.052	0.034
	(0.213)	(0.298)
Constant	−5.200*	−12.242
	(2.019)	(8.008)
χ^2	18.42**	18.38**
Log-likelihood	−90.11	−26.77
Pseudo R^2	0.05	0.08
N	845	603

Note: Robust standard errors appear in parentheses.
Significance levels refer to two-tailed tests.
$*p \leq .05$, $**p \leq .01$, $***p \leq .001$

trol variables; they offer little in the way of statistical improvement, but they are important to include on theoretical grounds.

Battle Fatalities

Another way of assessing the severity of conflicts is to investigate the battle fatalities incurred in a given dispute, although such an analysis overlaps with the last section, where I examined whether interdependence affected the likelihood of dyads falling within the highest category of conflict severity. Here, I examine whether they tend to fall within the higher categories or are distributed relatively equally across categories. It may be the case that dyads are equally likely to fall within high and low ranges of conflict severity. This would be consistent with the view that interdependence entails competing forces of peace and conflict, neither of which dominates the overall equation.

I use an ordered logit specification to examine whether interdependence increases the likelihood that dyads will experience higher levels of battle fatalities. This analysis provides a finer gradation of the various ranges of battle deaths experienced in a conflict, compared to the previous analyses of war. Positive coefficients mean that dyads are more likely to experience conflicts with high numbers of battle fatalities, rather than low numbers of fatalities. It is possible that interdependent dyads are equally likely to experience wars and to experience conflicts with low fatalities.

Table 7 reports the results of an analysis employing the partner-dependence measures, while table 8 reports the results of the economy-dependence measures. For the partner-based measures, I find that the interdependence index is statistically significant and positive. This means that high levels of interdependence, associated with high salience and symmetry, increase the likelihood that dyads will experience more severe conflicts. Salience and symmetry alone do not appear to have an independent effect on battle deaths, but their joint effect is significant. Obviously, this contradicts the assumption that interdependence constrains violent behavior. Instead, the findings appear more consistent with the view that conflicts are more intense when they arise in highly interdependent relationships.

Among the control variables, I also find that contiguous and allied dyads are more likely to experience severe conflicts. This may not be surprising if we consider these factors to represent other forms of interdependence—namely, geographical and military interdependence. Surprisingly, relative capabilities have no significant effect on battle fatalities, despite the tendency of conflict theorists to place a heavy emphasis on capabilities in determining conflict behavior. The lack of significance may result from two equally plausible scenarios that operate and whose effect might cancel each other out, in statistical terms. First, we can imagine that highly unequal power might result in high battle deaths, as a result of the stronger power's greater ability to inflict damage on a weak state. At the same time, relatively equal balances of power may result in more intractable conflicts, resulting in greater battle deaths. Perhaps a more surprising finding is the fact that joint democracy has a positive, but insignificant effect on battle fatalities. Given the proliferation of findings that jointly democratic dyads are more peaceful than other dyads, I would expect to find a significant negative effect on battle fatalities. The finding here, however, poses a less formidable challenge to the democratic peace

TABLE 7. INTERDEPENDENCE AND BATTLE FATALITIES, 1870–1992 (USING PARTNER-DEPENDENCE MEASURES)

Variable	Coefficient	Robust SE	z	p
Salience$_{t-1}$	3.210	2.917	1.100	0.271
Symmetry$_{t-1}$	−0.389	1.337	−0.291	0.771
Interdependence$_{t-1}$	0.230	0.084	2.723	0.006
Contiguity$_{t-1}$	0.689	0.244	2.821	0.005
Joint democracy$_{t-1}$	0.004	0.004	1.173	0.241
Alliance$_{t-1}$	0.369	0.204	1.812	0.070
Relative capabilities$_{t-1}$	−0.093	0.070	−1.322	0.186
Cut Point 1	1.741	1.346		
Cut Point 2	2.671	1.365		
Cut Point 3	3.300	1.367		
Cut Point 4	3.935	1.351		
Cut Point 5	3.991	1.353		
Cut Point 6	4.112	1.356		

χ^2	24.9***
Log-likelihood	−528.97
Pseudo R^2	0.02
N	780

Note: Significance levels refer to two-tailed tests.
***$p \leq .001$

proposition than that provided by Senese (1997), who finds a positive relationship between joint democracy and conflict intensity.

The findings reported in table 8 reveal that economy dependence does not appear to affect the battle fatality level. Obviously, this signifies that differences in empirical findings may result when employing alternative measures of interdependence. There are no compelling theoretical reasons to expect such differences. It may be the case that high partner-dependence tends to be more strongly associated with multiple forms of dependency compared to high economy dependence. As mentioned earlier, economy dependence will be higher for states that have lower GDP values. Again, it is unclear whether the differences in findings produced with alternative measures of dependence result from variations in sample size or composition or whether they result from real variations that exist between these types of interdependence. Perhaps more relevant to the conclusions about these findings is the fact that neither form of dependence offers a constraint to severe conflicts. Interdependence may not

TABLE 8.   INTERDEPENDENCE AND BATTLE FATALITIES, 1948–92 (USING ECONOMY-DEPENDENCE MEASURES)

Variable	Coefficient	Robust SE	z	p
Salience$_{t-1}$	−24.636	21.174	−1.163	0.245
Symmetry$_{t-1}$	−5.189	5.192	−0.999	0.318
Interdependence$_{t-1}$	−0.019	0.083	−0.225	0.822
Contiguity$_{t-1}$	1.457***	0.417	3.492	0.000
Joint democracy$_{t-1}$	0.006	0.004	1.299	0.194
Alliance$_{t-1}$	0.216	0.233	0.927	0.354
Relative capabilities$_{t-1}$	−0.100	0.087	−1.145	0.252
Cut Point 1	−2.576	5.041		
Cut Point 2	−1.494	5.047		
Cut Point 3	−0.753	5.039		
Cut Point 4	0.378	5.012		
Cut Point 5	0.534	5.006		
Cut Point 6	0.719	5.003		
χ^2	21.21***			
Log-likelihood	−373.92			
Pseudo R^2	0.04			
N	558			

Note: Significance levels refer to two-tailed tests.
***$p \leq .001$

increase the likelihood of severe disputes in the face of economic dependence, but it also will not decrease their likelihood.

The findings provide evidence of the competing forces that arise in interdependent relationships. Interdependent dyads may be equally likely to experience high and low battle fatalities, depending upon the type of interdependence analyzed. More important, it appears that cooperation and intense conflict may coexist in such relationships. The enhanced ability to achieve negotiated settlements of conflict is an indication that close ties can give rise to bonds conducive to cooperative conflict resolution. Yet, these mechanisms are not sufficient to preclude dyads from experiencing intense conflict. One might assume that intense conflicts provide an added impetus to seek negotiated settlements to conflicts; however, there appears to be no relationship between the intensity of a conflict and the settlement process. Of the 47 wars included in the sample of 1,591 disputes, 15 experienced negotiated settlements, while 32 did not. For nonwar disputes, 234 were negotiated, while 1,310 were not. Trade does appear to offer incentives or enhanced means for negotiating conflicts, but it does not appear to represent a constraint to the use of force.

CONCLUSION

Despite the importance ascribed to balanced dependence in economic and social theories, the findings appear to offer more support to the view that it is the *extensiveness of linkages,* rather than their symmetrical or asymmetrical nature, that influences the evolution of disputes. Moreover, extensive ties appear to contribute to competing forces in international relations, whereby both cooperation and conflict may coexist. High interdependence may aid in achieving negotiated resolutions to conflicts, but it does not appear to prevent their outbreak or escalation.

What may be equally surprising from the empirical results presented thus far is that economic relationships appear to have as much, if not more, of an impact on the conflict process as most of the factors traditionally believed to play a significant role. No evidence is provided to corroborate claims that jointly democratic dyads are less likely to engage in intense forms of conflict. The transmission of cultural norms and the establishment of institutional mechanisms to mediate conflict, in conjunction with the economic disincentives associated with extensive trade ties, appear to have little effect in inhibiting the escalation of conflict.

Again, to understand why familiarity breeds contempt, it is useful to consider the arguments advanced in the psychological and sociological theories describing the dynamics of close relationships. As discussed in chapter 2, the liberal peace presumes that commonalties foster peace. However, intense conflict is often found within groups united by commonalties.

Why would we expect intense conflict in interdependent relationships? One way to think about this is to imagine the differing expectations present in close relationships. States may have different (i.e., higher) expectations for their allies than their adversaries or neutral parties. Leaders might expect friends to act in a manner more consistent with their preferences. The reference point for allies and adversaries differs, resulting in greater discontent when the actions of allies depart from preferred outcomes. For example, when a close trading partner fails to respond to demands for a particular action, the gap between expectations and actual outcomes will be much greater than when an adversary ignores the same demands. Adversaries are expected to act in a manner inconsistent with one's preferences, while friends are expected to compromise or acquiesce to requests or demands.

Feelings of betrayal may be greater when there is a divergence of expectations on the part of a close partner. This might explain why civil wars are more intense than other conflicts; the expectations citizens maintain toward their own government and their fellow citizens are greater than those anticipated from foreigners. For example, the animosity expressed against the enemy within is likely to be more intense than that expressed toward an external enemy (Coser 1956, chap. 4). This suggests that becoming more interdependent may be positive when the relationship is harmonious, but once conflicts arise, they may become more intense. Interdependent actors may have a tendency to suppress hostilities in the interest of preserving the relationship, but once a conflict breaks out there may be an outpouring of animosity, leading to more intense disputes. The review of critical theories in chapter 2 provides some explanation for the many sources of tension that may result among trading partners, but these sources of tension need not be the cause of the particular dispute. They may, however, contribute to the intensity of non-trade-related conflicts.

The analyses conducted in this chapter raise some interesting questions that require further exploration. It is clear that interdependence entails both negative and positive aspects. These dimensions are seen at all stages of the conflict process. What is less clear is how to minimize the negative consequences of interdependence and to strengthen the positive effects. The predictions of liberal theories with respect to conflict occurrence failed to uncover the mystery of why interdependent states were more likely to engage in disputes. This was to some extent explained by the guidance provided by critics of liberal thought. Still, it appears that further clarity is achieved by moving beyond economic interpretations of the trade-conflict relationship to incorporate psychological and sociological theories of close relationships. From these theories, we understand that interdependence can entail cooperation and intense conflict. Yet, further exploration of their relevance for international relations scholarship is required.

Chapter 5

ALTERNATIVE LEVELS OF
ANALYSIS: THE NATION-STATE
AND THE SYSTEM

Throughout this study, I have focused on the impact of trade on dyadic relationships in order to look within the international system to determine whether variations in the trade-conflict relationship exist. However, people tend to portray discussions about trade as equally applicable to all relationships, including those between people, classes, communities, and the global community as a whole. Liberals have spent a considerable amount of time focusing on the impact that commerce has on transforming states. For this reason, it is important to consider whether states that engage more heavily in trade are more peaceful than others. In addition, while it is difficult to draw close linkages between global forces and the actions of individual states within any given relationship, some consideration of systemwide interdependence is useful. Thus, in this chapter, I seek to look beyond trade's impact on dyadic relationships to assess its impact on states and the system.

Conflict researchers provide a valuable lesson in revealing that factors associated with conflict may vary at different levels of analysis. For example, researchers investigating the "democratic peace" proposition (that increased democracy promotes peace) have identified different relationships between democracy and conflict at the monadic, dyadic, and system levels of analysis (Gleditsch and Hegre 1997; Ray and Wang 1998). The same may be true with respect to commerce, where the impact may vary at alternative levels of analysis. In this chapter, I examine the extent to which the trade-promotes-peace hypothesis enjoys empirical support at the state and system levels of analysis.

A major difficulty in assessing trade's impact across different levels of analysis arises from the ambiguity about the conditions that define trade dependence or interdependence. As I discussed previously, scholars disagree about the meaning and operationalization of interdependence at the dyadic level. That problem is compounded when I expand my domain of inquiry beyond the dyadic level of analysis. Rather than definitively resolving the issue of the most appropriate measure of trade dependence, I explore a number of ways in which we might conceive of trade's impact on conflict behavior at the monadic and system levels.

The review of theoretical literature presented in chapter 2 showed that classical liberals assumed that trade would have an impact on the conflict behavior of states. Liberals assume that trading states are more peaceful than those states that refrain from trade. They assume that this pacifying effect on state behavior arises from both the economic motivations to refrain from conflict and the positive social transformations, including, for some, moral elevation, presumed to be associated with participating in commerce. Despite the wealth of literature outlining trade's positive effect, scholars have provided little investigative research into the question of whether trading states are more peaceful than other states. In fact, Domke (1988) provides the only comprehensive empirical study of the impact of trade dependence on war involvement. Domke finds that states that depend on trade relative to national production are less likely to become involved in wars than are other states. Scholars seem content to accept Domke's monadic-level findings without further exploration, despite some obvious limitations in his research design. For example, Domke focuses exclusively on years in which wars occur, a research strategy that may be biased for not considering all years (nonwar years, as well as war years). That is, years in which wars occur may be different, with respect to trading relationships, than years in which no war occurs. In addition, Domke considers only the bivariate relationship between trade dependence and war involvement and fails to control for other factors believed to be associated with both trade and conflict. Whether or not one accepts Domke's basic research design, his monadic-level findings deserve further consideration to determine whether trading states are more peaceful than other states. In this study, I extend his analysis by considering whether trading states are less likely than others to participate in other forms of militarized conflict, including, but not limited to wars.

Research Design

I wish to examine whether the liberal proposition that trade promotes peace applies to a state's participation in international trade. Does increased trade reduce a state's conflict proneness? To examine this question in a manner consistent with my dyadic analyses, I consider the relationship between a state's total trade and its propensity to engage in militarized interstate disputes. Here, my unit of observation is the individual state at each year in the sample, rather than the dyad. I examine the period 1870–1992 in my initial analysis, but must confine the analyses to the post–World War II period, when measures of GDP are introduced.

The Dependent Variable: Militarized Interstate Disputes

Once again, the MID data set is used to measure the dependent variable—conflict. Here I examine the total number of disputes in which a state participates in a given year. Given the nature of the dependent variable, it is necessary that I use a method of statistical analysis appropriate for analyzing count variables. Thus, I use negative binomial analysis to estimate the rate at which disputes occur per year. Negative binomial regression is used, rather than the more commonly used Poisson regression, when the sample may be heterogeneous—when the rate of event occurrence varies. Poisson regression analysis, on the other hand, assumes homogeneity of the sample (see King 1989, esp. 122). The negative binomial regression provides an estimate of an alpha coefficient to determine whether heterogeneity is present in the sample. When estimating a negative binomial model, a Poisson regression model is first estimated. When the alpha coefficient is statistically significant, the results from the negative binomial model should be used; otherwise, the Poisson regression estimates are used.

Independent Variables: Trade Dependence

First, I consider whether states with extensive foreign trade are more peaceful than states with limited trade and measure a state's total trade as the sum of its imports and exports. This assumes that the benefits of trade and the potential threat of trade losses are similar across states and vary only according to the absolute value of trade. But a given value of total trade may be more important for states with smaller economies, who are less able than large states to substitute domestic production for foreign trade. Therefore, I introduce a control for economic size (measured by GDP) into the estimated model specification in the second analysis. Since GDP figures are not readily available for most states in the pre–World War II period, the analyses that include this variable must be confined to the post–World War II era. In my third analysis, I employ a ratio measure of trade dependence that is similar to Domke's (1988), whose measure of trade dependence evaluates total exports relative to GDP. However, I evaluate total trade relative to GDP. I include both imports and exports in my measure of trade dependence, because I believe that an exclusive focus on exports reflects the mercantilist bias of favoring export over import flows, rather than the liberal recognition that each flow is important to the overall economy.

The trade-dependence ratio is similar in some respects to controlling for GDP by including it as a separate variable. Yet, the approaches do differ. The ratio variable may mask the separate independent influence of trade and GDP. Similarly, it might mask the separate effects of trade dependence and GDP alone. For this reason, I include a control for GDP in my third analysis. Controlling for GDP in the trade-dependence model is also important, since trade dependence is negatively associated with GDP. States with large economies are less dependent on foreign trade relative to national production than are states with small economies.

My first measure, total trade, is reported in current U.S. dollars. It is necessary to control for the purchasing power of the dollar over time, since the value of a dollar in 1950 is higher than a dollar in 1992. To convert current to real U.S. dollars, I employ the U.S. Consumer Price Index with 1967 as the base year.[1] Despite the prevalent tendency to apply the U.S. CPI Index to other states, there are limitations to this approach. Price variations in other countries might be very different than in the United States, so the CPI Index is only a rough estimate of price variations for other states. Unfortunately, there are few viable options for standardizing global trade figures over space and time. Thus, the trade values must be considered an estimated trade index. Hence, Total Trade in the models that follow is defined as (Imports + Exports)/CPI_{US}. The same procedure is applied to convert GDP in current dollars to constant dollars.

Control Variables

I control for those factors that I previously argued were associated with both trade and conflict, including contiguity, regime type, alliances, and power, but here I transform these variables to their monadic level. We can imagine several ways in which these control variables might be applicable to a monadic-level analysis. With respect to contiguity at the dyadic level, I argued that contiguous states are more likely to trade and more likely to get involved in conflict. At the national level, those states with numerous bordering states may have a greater opportunity to engage in trade and may also have more opportunities to engage in conflict. Thus, the number of bordering states a given state has should be positively associated with trade and conflict. For this reason, I introduce a control variable for contiguity that I measure as the total number of states that border a given state (i.e., how many states are directly contiguous to it).

My previous discussion about the democratic peace suggested that theories about the peacefulness of democracies are generally cast at all levels of analysis, although empirical findings may not bear that out. Since wealthy, more industrialized states tend to be more democratic than developing states and also tend to participate more in foreign trade, it is important to control for regime type. To measure regime type, I use the *Polity III* democracy score minus the Autocracy score, plus ten.

As discussed previously, alliance ties may affect conflict and trade patterns. States tend to trade with allies and refrain from trade with adversaries. One might reason that the more allies a state has, the more opportunities it has to trade with those states. To measure alliance ties, I include a count of the number of alliances a given state has in a given year. Power is also relevant for a monadic-level analysis, since powerful states play an active role in international trade and also are more likely to participate in conflict. Thus, it is important to control for the power of a nation. To do so, I use the COW CINC score for the nation in a given year. Similar to my approach in my dyadic-level analyses, here I employ a one-year lag for all of the independent variables.

EMPIRICAL FINDINGS

The results for the first analysis of the peacefulness of trading states are reported in table 9, which examines whether states that conduct a large amount of foreign trade are more peaceful than those that refrain from trade. The findings reveal a statistically significant positive relationship between total trade and conflict. Within the context of the negative binomial analysis, a positive coefficient means that states with high levels of trade have a higher rate of dispute involvement than those with lower levels of trade. Clearly, this finding contradicts the notion that trading states are more peaceful than other states. One might easily argue that the total-trade variable simply highlights the fact that powerful states trade a lot and are also more likely to engage in conflicts. The control for capabilities should account for the impact of power among nations in the sample and should allow me to estimate the independent contributions of power and trade to the rate of conflict involvement. Not surprisingly, the findings reveal that more powerful states, as indicated by the capability variable, have higher rates of dispute involvement.

The other control variables provide few surprises. States that share many borders have higher rates of dispute involvement than those that have fewer bordering countries, supporting the general view that contiguity provides more opportunities for disputes to arise. I find support for the argument that democratic states are more peaceful than other states. The negative coefficient for democracy reveals that states with higher levels of democratic characteristics have lower rates of dispute involvement than those states that are less democratic. Although alliance ties were found to increase the likelihood of conflict in dyadic relationships, alliance ties at the monadic level appear to be associated with lower rates of conflict involvement.

As discussed previously, total trade is not only positively correlated with power, it is also positively associated with economic size and wealth. Economically strong states play a very active role in international trade and have higher volumes of trade than poor states. It is, therefore, useful to determine whether the relationship between total trade and conflict

TABLE 9. TOTAL TRADE AND DISPUTE PARTICIPATION, 1870–1992

Variable	Coefficient	Robust SE	z	p
Total trade$_{t-1}$	0.000007	0.000001	6.591	0.000
Contiguity$_{t-1}$	0.105878	0.007582	13.965	0.000
Democracy$_{t-1}$	−0.013258	0.003310	−4.005	0.000
Alliances$_{t-1}$	−0.007618	0.001923	−3.961	0.000
Capabilities$_{t-1}$	0.086485	0.004026	21.484	0.000
Constant	−1.430376	0.056014	−25.536	0.000
lnalpha constant[a]	0.212311	0.072721	2.920	0.004
alpha	1.236533	0.089922	1.072	1.426

[a]lnalpha constant = ln(alpha)
$N = 8{,}210$
Log likelihood = −7,034.37, $\chi^2(5) = 1{,}117.43$, $p = 0.0000$
Pseudo $R^2 = 0.07$

involvement persists when I introduce a statistical control for economic strength or a proxy for wealth. It is true that wealth may be considered a central component of power, and I have controlled for power. But the capability indicator used here incorporates other sources of power (military, demographic, and economic) and is not identical to a measure of economic strength. Wealth can affect total trade, and it might also affect conflict (Bremer 1992b). Two equally plausible propositions emerge about the relationship between wealth and conflict. One could argue that wealthy states are less likely to engage in conflict, since they are more likely to be satisfied with the status quo that maintains their economic position. On the other hand, if we assume that conflicts of interest are a natural part of international relations, we might assume that wealthy states are better equipped with the resources to engage in disputes when conflicts of interest cannot be resolved through other means. According to this argument, states with high GDPs should have a higher rate of conflict involvement.

In the analysis presented in table 10, I introduce a control for GDP when analyzing the relationship between total trade and national conflict involvement. Once I control for economic size, the impact of total trade on conflict involvement becomes statistically insignificant. What does this mean? We see from the statistically significant

TABLE 10. TOTAL TRADE AND DISPUTE PARTICIPATION, 1948–92

Variable	Coefficient	Robust SE	z	p
Total trade$_{t-1}$	−0.000003	0.000003	−1.152	0.249
GDP$_{t-1}$	0.000002	0.000001	2.786	0.005
Contiguity$_{t-1}$	0.115130	0.011970	9.619	0.000
Democracy$_{t-1}$	−0.007374	0.003821	−1.930	0.054
Alliances$_{t-1}$	−0.016743	0.002621	−6.388	0.000
Capabilities$_{t-1}$	0.075062	0.012255	6.125	0.000
Constant	−1.337631	0.072216	−18.523	0.000
lnalpha constant[a]	0.092353	0.098600	0.937	0.349
alpha	1.096752	0.108140	0.904	1.331

[a]lnalpha constant = ln(alpha)
$N = 4,794$
Log likelihood = −4,190.8, $\chi^2(6) = 679.35$, $p = 0.0000$
Pseudo $R^2 = 0.08$

coefficient for GDP that states with larger GDPs have a higher rate of conflict involvement than those with smaller GDPs. The fact that the total trade indicator is no longer significant means that the relationship observed previously can be explained largely by the different rates of conflict involvement between wealthy and poor states, rather than by large and small trading volumes of states. This finding provides little support to the view that trading states are more peaceful, but it also does not directly support the argument that they are more conflictual. If, on the other hand, we consider the liberal arguments that trade contributes to wealth and economic efficiency, and then consider the fact that economic power increases the rate of conflict involvement, we may view trade as having an indirect effect on conflict involvement. The control variables in this analysis continue to reveal the same predictions found previously.

Finally, I argued that trade might serve as a more effective deterrent to conflict when states are heavily dependent on trade relative to domestic production. Thus, I estimate the influence of trade dependence when evaluated as the ratio of total trade to GDP. Trade dependence conceived in this manner tends to be inversely associated with GDP. That is, states with large economies are less reliant on foreign trade and are better able to substitute domestic production for foreign resources and markets. It is useful to consider the separate effects on conflict involvement of trade dependence and GDP, so the following analysis includes measures of each of these variables.

Table 11 presents the results of my analysis of trade dependence and national conflict. Here is evidence that trade dependence at the national level may have a pacifying effect on national conflict involvement. The statistically significant negative coefficient for trade dependence reveals that states that are heavily dependent on foreign trade have lower rates of conflict involvement than those who are less dependent. This suggests that *it is the importance of trade for a country's economy, rather than the mere volume of trade, that determines whether trade is an effective deterrent to conflict.* The finding that states with a high trade dependence are more peaceful may not appear surprising if we consider the fact that such states tend to be the less powerful ones in the system. However, the controls for wealth and power should account for such variations across nations and allow us to observe the independent influence of trade dependence on conflict involvement. The GDP and capabilities variables tell us that

TABLE 11. TRADE DEPENDENCE AND DISPUTE
PARTICIPATION, 1948–92

Variable	Coefficient	Robust SE	z	p
Trade dependence$_{t-1}$	−0.503827	0.089586	−5.624	0.000
GDP$_{t-1}$	0.000001	0.000000	5.110	0.000
Contiguity$_{t-1}$	0.104862	0.009625	10.895	0.000
Democracy$_{t-1}$	−0.007855	0.003801	−2.067	0.039
Alliances$_{t-1}$	−0.017585	0.002536	−6.935	0.000
Capabilities$_{t-1}$	0.070782	0.008850	7.998	0.000
Constant lnalpha[a]	−1.028776	0.083553	−12.313	0.000
Constant	0.051370	0.099101	0.518	0.604
alpha	1.052712	0.104325	0.867	1.278

[a]lnalpha constant = ln(alpha)
$N = 4794$
Log likelihood = −4173.04, $\chi^2(6) = 701.57$, $p = 0.0000$
Pseudo $R^2 = 0.08$

wealthy and powerful states have higher rates of conflict involvement than other states.

In sum, this analysis provides the first sign that the liberal hypothesis may enjoy support at the monadic level of analysis. Of course, if I combine this finding with the previous dyadic-level analysis, I might conclude that countries that are more dependent upon trade have lower rates of conflict involvement, but when they do choose to engage in conflict, they are more likely to do so with their most important trading partners. Moreover, the finding that wealthy states have higher rates of conflict involvement suggests that trade may have an indirect effect on increasing the conflict proneness of nations. If liberals are correct in their assumption that trade contributes to wealth, then increased trade may eventually lead to a state's increased ability to engage in conflict.

SYSTEM LEVEL

Having found evidence that trade's impact on conflict may vary at the monadic and dyadic levels of analysis, depending upon how one measures trade dependence, I consider what this means for the global system as a whole. An extensive analysis of the system level factors affecting conflict is beyond the scope of this study, but a few comments are in order with respect to the applicability of the trade-promotes-peace hypothesis to the system level. Anyone with regular exposure to news media would find it difficult to ignore the constant references to globalization and expressions of the opinion that we live in an increasingly interdependent world. Clichés about the shrinking world have been common for several decades, but appear to be taking on added importance in the popular press. References to globalization imply more than the expansion of world trade. When we think about what is meant by the process of globalization, it becomes clear that focusing exclusively on trade ties underplays the many ways in which the global economy has become more integrated over time. Discussions of global interdependence tend to be identified with the weakening of national borders; the rapid movement of capital, goods, services, and people; and the ripple effects throughout the system of actions or events in one area of the globe.

Still, trade remains a key element in the process of globalization. Moreover, classical liberals advocated the creation of a global economy through trade as means to promote peace in the international system. Thus, it is important to consider whether the expansion of global trade has brought greater peace to the international system. People react to the idea of globalization with the same diversity of opinions and passion of sentiments as they do to the notions of interdependence discussed at the dyadic level. Globalization is credited with contributing to global wealth, integration, and world peace. On the other hand, it is blamed for problems such as unemployment, inequality between and within nations, cultural imperialism, environmental degradation, and conflict.

Since foreign trade is an important dimension of the globalization process, we might ask what the expansion of world trade has meant for international conflict on a global scale. Data availability on the world's total trade figures are difficult to obtain, but Maddison (1995, 239) provides a comprehensive series of global exports for most of the period analyzed in this study. Figure 3 illustrates the growth of global exports during the period 1881–1992, excluding the years surrounding World War I and World War II (Maddison 1995, 239).

Does the expansion of trade correspond to the creation of a more peaceful world? Scholars remain divided on the relative peace or conflict in the international system today compared to previous periods in history. In part, a scholar's assessment about the state of the world centers on the manner in which she or he defines the most dangerous forms of conflict. Forbes provides an interesting response to the anticipated criticisms of Montesquieu's notion that commerce will lead to peace:

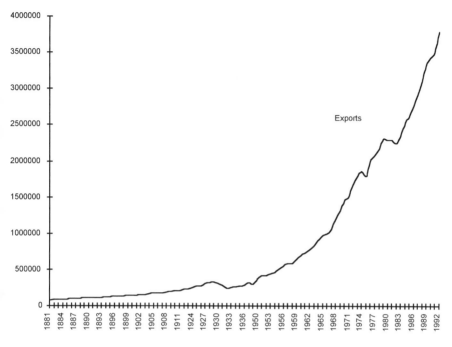

FIG. 3. World exports (in 1990 U.S. dollars)

Hasn't Montesquieu's theory been disproved by events? Commerce has grown enormously since the eighteenth century, but the world has become more violent. Indeed, the twentieth century has probably witnessed more suffering from nationalist wars and other eruptions of ethnic violence than any previous century, and not just because technology has made war more destructive. Since the eighteenth century, aggressive nationalism and racism closely akin to it have been added to the older causes of war. The new factors seem to have grown with commerce, and they have generated conflicts within as well as between states. (1997, 3)

There are undoubtedly many systemic factors that contribute to the variations in conflict found within the international system. It would be difficult to argue that the variations in conflict within the system are primarily determined by the growth of commerce. Waltz (1979), for example, argues that the concentration of power in the system remains the central determinant of peace or conflict within the international system. Still, it is interesting to consider how the incidence of militarized inter-state disputes, the type of conflict I have considered thus far, has changed over time at the system level, given the general growth in commerce.

Several scholars have recently provided extensive analyses of the general trends in militarized conflict within the system over time (Jones, Bremer, and Singer 1996; Maoz 1996). Each reveals an upward trend in militarized disputes over time that, in part, corresponds to the increase in the number of states within the system. Estimates of trends in disputes and wars systemwide will vary, depending upon whether one looks at the onset of new conflicts or participation in ongoing conflicts and whether one controls for the number of states in the international system. Figure 4 illustrates the number of new disputes and wars beginning each year during the period 1870–1992.

There appears to be an upward trend in the frequency of new disputes, but there is no apparent trend in their severity and magnitude, as indicated by the war measure. In figure 5, I control for the total number of states in the system, and the upward trend in disputes disappears. We might assume that having more states in the system leads to more disputes, since disputes require the participation of states. However, a small number of states account for the majority of disputes, which means that having more states in the system need not entail more disputes (Maoz 1996).

Reaching definitive conclusions about trends in the frequency of conflict over time is difficult, since disputes and wars are relatively rare events. It is difficult to say that the world has become a much more peaceful place over time, as a result of the expansion of commerce. Yet, it is equally difficult to argue that militarized conflict has become more pervasive with the growth of trade. If anything, civil wars have become a greater threat than interstate wars over time (Hughes 1997, 111). Although domestic conflict is not the focus of this investigation, it is important to consider the fact that groups within nations, which are assumed to be more interdependent than interstate groups, continue to face increasing threats of armed conflict. The optimistic reader could interpret the infrequency of war as a sign that the growth of the global economy has produced a more peaceful world. The more pessimistic reader might note that militarized conflict continues to plague the international community, despite the growth of systemwide interdependence.

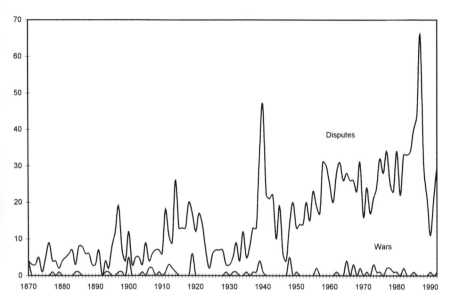

F I G . 4. Number of new militarized disputes and wars per year, 1870–1992

Of course, just as scholars disagree about world peace, scholars also disagree about systemic interdependence.

As mentioned, Kenneth Waltz (1979) argues that the world is less
interdependent in the post–World War II period than it was in previous
periods in history. Furthermore, he maintains that decreased interdependence has a pacifying effect, since the extensive contacts associated with
high interdependence increase the opportunities for conflicts to arise.
Waltz's conception of systemic interdependence differs from that discussed previously and is worth considering here, given the prominence
that some international relations scholars accord to his work. He
explains:

> When I say that interdependence is tighter or looser, I am saying
> something about the international system, with systems-level charac-
> teristics defined, as ever, by the situation of the great powers. In any
> international-political system some of the major and minor states are

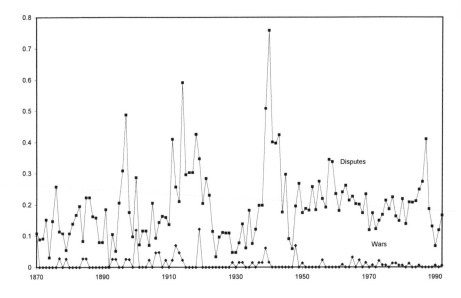

FIG. 5. Frequency of new conflicts per year, controlling for system size,
1870–1992

closely interdependent; others are heavily dependent. The system, however, is tightly or loosely interdependent according to the relatively high or low dependence of the great powers. Interdependence is therefore looser now than it was before and between the two world wars of this century. (144–45)

Waltz argues that we cannot talk about interdependence without recognizing the inequalities in power that exist in the world (1979, 152–53).

The common conception of interdependence is appropriate only if the inequalities of nations are fast lessening and losing their political significance. If the inequality of nations is still the dominant political fact of international life, then interdependence remains low. (152)

Seldom has the discrepancy been wider between the homogeneity suggested by 'interdependence' and the heterogeneity of the world we live in. A world composed of greatly unequal units is scarcely an interdependent one. A world in which a few states can take care of themselves quite well and most states cannot hope to do so is scarcely an interdependent one. (159)

Today the myth of interdependence both obscures the realities of international politics and asserts a false belief about the conditions that promote peace, as World War I conclusively showed. (158)

We see that Waltz's notion of systemic interdependence is tied to the relationships between the major powers. At the same time, he recognizes that the notion of an "interdependent" world is illusory, when such inequalities exist as those between rich and poor states. While Waltz looks beyond trade ties and considers other forms of economic interdependence, such as investment ties, his analysis is still telling.[2] In fact, his analysis underscores the importance of looking beyond trade ties when evaluating global interdependence. Here, my intent in focusing on trade ties is to shed light on the prominent theories about trading relationships. At the same time, when we talk about interdependence, particularly on a global scale, it is difficult to ignore the many factors that give rise to such relationships. Still, we can consider Waltz's proposition with respect to trade relations. In fact, his approach offers a medium between my dyadic approach and a system level perspective, since Waltz's definition of systemic interdependence is tied to dyadic relationships between major powers. My intent here is descriptive, examining whether Waltz's concept of interdependence explains the patterns of trade and conflict over time and to determine what this has meant for major power conflicts.

In general, major powers were more dependent on their major power partners in the pre–World War I period than in any period since that time. Here, I mean that major power states conducted a much higher share of their total trade with each other; major powers were more reliant on their major power trading partners than they are reliant on any states today. The question remains whether dependence between major power states was significant prior to the outbreak of the major wars. Liberals claim that it is the absence of trade ties that results in war, rather than the presence of such ties. If we consider the periods before the major world wars of the twentieth century, we see that both patterns occurred—states were dependent upon those states that became allies and adversaries in war. Is one pattern more prevalent? Does Waltz's notion of systemic inter-dependence tell us anything about the outbreak of war in different eras?

In this descriptive analysis, I look at trade dependence for each of the major powers in turn during the period 1870 until 1913 (see appendix B for displays of these data). These figures are rough estimates of the extent to which major powers relied upon each other before and after a major power war. Trade statistics for earlier periods in history, as well as exchange rate data, are less exact than in later periods.[3] Nevertheless, we can still see whether the patterns of trade appear to mirror the alliances formed around the periods of the world wars.

Let's first consider the case of Germany and those states we consider Germany's chief allies and adversaries in the period surrounding World War I. Prior to World War I, Germany depended most heavily on Russia and Britain. In 1913, Germany's most important trading partner in terms of share of total trade was Russia, who accounted for more than 13 percent of Germany's total trade. Britain and the United States followed, with both states accounting for approximately 12 percent of Germany's total trade. France's dyadic trade with Germany accounted for approximately 7 percent of the total trade. Clearly, the importance of these trade relationships did little to stem the tide of war. Germany also conducted significant trade with its allies. Austria-Hungary accounted for approximately 9 percent of Germany's total trade, and Italy accounted for approximately 4 percent. There is some variation in Germany's level of trade dependence during the period 1870–1913, but no sharp divergence in the basic composition of trade partners. In general, it would be difficult to look at Germany's trade patterns and argue that trade dependence prevented war between allied or adversarial states.

Were other major powers equally dependent upon those states whom they would engage in war or beside whom they would fight? Do the patterns of dependence appear to reflect the major alliances of the period? Austria-Hungary's trade statistics are less complete than the other major powers, but it is still possible to consider the evidence that exists for this state.

Austria-Hungary's most important trading partner in the pre–World War I period was Germany, accounting for an average of 30 to 40 percent of Austria-Hungary's total trade. Clearly, this is consistent with the alliance patterns of World War I. Italy ranks second in importance. Russia and Britain account for approximately 4 to 5 percent of Austria-Hungary's total trade in 1913. Dependence on the United States declines to approximately 3 percent of total trade in 1913, compared to approximately 6 percent in 1910. France's share of Austria-Hungary's total trade also appears to decline after 1900 (6.7 percent) to about 2.5 percent. It appears that trade dependence may reflect emerging alliance patterns and foreshadow divides between adversaries in war, but there are no apparent patterns that would lead one to conclude that trade helped prevent war, unless one were to conclude that the allies remained at peace, because of the trade that existed between them.

In the pre–World War I era, Russia is actually more dependent upon Germany than Germany is on Russia. From 1870 through 1913, trade with Germany ranged between 18 and 46 percent of Russia's total trade, with dependence at around 45 percent in 1913. Russia was also heavily dependent upon Britain during this period, with trade dependence at an average of about 20 percent of total trade. France rates third for Russia's dependence, averaging approximately 8 percent during the period. Russia's dependence on the United States rose during the period, from less than 2 percent before 1905 to more than 4 percent after 1905. Russian dependence on Austria-Hungary varied within a small margin around 4 percent, declining slightly in the period leading up to World War I. A similar pattern is observed with Russia's dependence on Italy; dependence grew after 1885, but varied within a small range around the 4 percent level witnessed on the eve of World War I. For Russia, there are no sharp variations in dependence levels with any one partner, other than the positive trend in dependence observed with Germany and the United States.

For Britain, trade dependence is most heavily concentrated on the United States, which accounts for 15 to 27 percent of Britain's total trade during the pre–World War I period. Germany ranks second in importance, with dependence ranging from about 10 to 11 percent of Britain's total trade prior to World War I. France ranks third in partner dependence for Britain, with approximately 7 percent of total trade, followed by Russia who accounts for approximately 5 percent of Britain's total trade in 1913. Italy follows in dependence rankings, accounting for approximately 3 percent of total trade. Austria-Hungary is the least significant partner for Britain among the major power group; dependence on this state declines to around 1 percent of total trade in 1913.

For France, the most important trading partner during the pre–World War I period analyzed here is Britain, but trade dependence declines after 1900 to about 14 percent in 1913. Germany ranks second for France, with dependence rising for most, but not all years, in the period analyzed, accounting for almost 12 percent of France's total trade in 1913. The United States is France's third most important partner, with nearly 11 percent of total trade in 1913, followed by Russia, with approximately 4 percent in 1913. Italy accounts for a little more than 3 percent of total trade in 1913 and Austria-Hungary a minor 1 percent.

For Italy, dependence on Germany is most significant; the dyadic relationship accounts for 16 percent of Italy's total trade in 1913. Dependence on Britain and the United States also appears to be increasing in the period leading up to World War I, where each accounts for nearly 13 percent of total trade in 1913. France accounts for approximately 8.5 percent of Italy's total trade in 1913, a slight decline from earlier years. Dependence on Austria-Hungary and Russia also appears to experience a slight decline during the period to the levels of 8 percent and 4.5 percent of total trade, respectively.

Since its arrival at major power status in 1899, the United States' most important trading partner is Britain, who accounts for over 20 percent of U.S. total trade during the period. Germany is also significant to the United States, with dependence rising to about 14 percent of the United States' total trade in 1913. Dependence on France accounts for approximately 7 percent of U.S. total trade, while Italy accounts for approximately 4 percent. Among the major powers not discussed in detail here (since it has no role in World War I), U.S. dependence on Japan is growing during this time and accounts for nearly 5 percent of total trade. Austria-Hungary accounts for only about 1 percent of the United States' total trade.

From these trade patterns, we see that dependence is high between the major powers that constituted the allies and adversaries in World War I. In general, the levels of dependence exhibited during the pre–World War I period are much higher than we see for major powers in later periods of the century. There is no clear indication that rising or declining dependence was associated with the alliance patterns of the war. Similarly, there is no evidence that only the interdependent dyads were belligerents. In some cases, a state was most dependent upon another state that would become its adversary in war. In other cases, dependence was highest with an ally. There is, however, general support here for the view that dependence was high for the major powers. To understand the relative levels of dependence, it is helpful to consider later periods of history. I turn now to the interwar period, to see how the state of interdependence among the major powers changed from the pre–World War I levels.

German dependence on other major powers appears high in 1920, but these figures may be less reliable than others, due to rapid fluctuations in exchange rates for Germany for this period and the difficulties this creates in converting local currencies to standardized international figures. For the interwar period, Germany's dependence on France, Russia, the United States, and Britain appears to decline significantly from the pre–World War I levels. Dependence on Japan and Italy, on the other hand, appears to increase, but not by a great extent. Aside from the cases of Italy and Japan, the general degree of trade dependence is much lower than that observed in the pre–World War I period.

Italy's dependence on most states also declines in the interwar period, with the exception of Germany. In fact, the degree of dependence on Germany is much higher than the levels observed in the pre–World War I period. This provides some indication that there was some consistency in alliance and trade patterns, but the relationship is not particularly precise, as shown in other major power relationships. For Italy, the rankings of trade partners by dependence levels remain similar to the pre–World War I period, but the general level of dependence is lower in all cases but Germany.

For Japan, trade dependence is highest in its relationship with the United States. Dependence on Britain is similar to the levels with Germany, but dependence on Germany is rising, while dependence on Britain is declining. Italy, France, and Russia each account for less than 1 percent of Japan's interwar total trade, which illustrates the fact that in most cases, the level of trade dependence in major power relations declined after World War I.

A comparison of Britain's level of dependence on the major powers in the pre–World War I and interwar periods provides further evidence that dependence between major powers declined. Once again, we see that the basic ranking of partner dependence is similar, with the United States the most important trading partner, followed by Germany, France, Russia, Italy, and Japan, but that the level of dependence on all states has dramatically dropped.

Turning to the case of Russia, we actually see instances of higher trade dependence in the interwar period than in the pre–World War I period. It appears that Russia's heavy trade dependence on Germany prior to the war was redirected toward other partners. The United States now tops Russia's list of important trading partners, and the degree of dependence is much higher than that observed prior to the war (ranging from 8 to 19 percent in the interwar period, compared to less than 5 percent prior to the war). Dependence on Britain is also increasing, while dependence on France, Italy, and Japan suggests a decline.

France's trade dependence on the major powers is also much lower in the interwar period than it was prior to World War I. On the eve of World War II, France is most dependent on the United States and Britain (each accounting for approximately 9 percent of France's total trade in 1938). France's trade dependence on the major powers is declining, with the exception of Russia; dependence levels are still much lower relative to the pre–World War I period.

U.S. dependence on other major powers is also lower in the interwar period than it was prior to World War I. Britain remains the most important partner, but dependence levels drop to only 13 percent of total trade in 1938, compared to 21 percent in 1913. Dependence on Germany declines significantly to 4 percent in 1938, compared to nearly 14 percent in 1913. Russia, on the other hand, represents a larger share of the United States' total trade in the interwar period than it did prior to World War I. In 1938, dyadic trade with Russia represents 2 percent of the United States' total trade, a figure larger than previous periods, but still not very significant. Dependence on Japan is also higher during this period, relative to the pre–World War I period, but declines from 9 percent to 8 percent during the period 1935 to 1938.

This brief review of major power trade dependence in the interwar period reveals that in general trade dependence was much lower than in the pre–World War I era. The war appears to have led to a reduced reliance on Germany for most states, with the exception of its allies. Here, there is a clearer distinction in the tendencies for dependence to be higher among allies than adversaries for the coming war, compared to the case in the pre–World War I era. However, the decline in dependence for the major powers was unable to stem the tide of war. Liberals, in fact, claim it contributed to the outbreak of war. What is clear is that the world wars occurred during periods in which major power trade dependence was relatively high and low. Similarly, dependence levels in some cases were high with both allies and adversaries, making it difficult to draw any definitive conclusions about the relationship between interdependence and war.

Regarding the argument that major powers are less dependent on each other in the post–World War II era than they were in previous eras, the indicators of partner dependence support that view. Again, we must recognize that Waltz (1979) referred to more than trade ties, but trade ties should be highly correlated with other forms of economic and even noneconomic bonds, if liberal theories about integration are correct. The major power club changes after World War II, just as it did after World War I. The main example Waltz cites as evidence of decreased interdependence is the case of the United States and the Soviet Union. Data on this dyadic relationship are limited until after 1980. The few figures that are available during the Cold War clearly indicate that U.S.-Russian trade ties were less salient relative to each state's total trade than they were in the pre–World War II period. It is interesting to note that after the publication of Waltz's book in 1979, Russia's trade dependence on the major powers increases. This undoubtedly relates to Russia's increased integration into the global economy, following the disintegration of the Soviet Union.

While U.S. dependence on Russia has grown, it remains insignificant, accounting for less than 1 percent of the United States' total trade. U.S. dependence on other major powers also remains low, with Britain, France, and China each accounting for less than 5 percent of the United States' total trade in 1992. Again, the dependence levels I find are much lower than they were in the past. For Britain, the United States remains the most important trading partner, but France is increasing in importance; British-French trade accounts for almost 10 percent of Britain's total trade in 1992, compared to 11 percent conducted with the United States. British dependence on China is also growing, but this dyadic relationship accounts for less than 1 percent of Britain's total trade, a figure comparable to Britain's dependence on Russia. The highest levels of dependence for any major power are found in China's dependence on the United States. In 1992, U.S. trade ties represented more than 21 percent of China's total trade. This level is extremely high compared to other trade ties between major powers in the post–World War II period and is similar to the levels of dependence observed between major powers in the pre–World War I era. We also see an increase in China's dependence on Russia, which accounts for about 4 percent of China's total trade.

In conclusion, interdependence—if conceived of as dependence between the major powers—has declined significantly over time. Many of the same patterns of the states upon whom one state depends most heavily persist for long periods of history, but the amount that any state is dependent upon another state has declined significantly relative to earlier periods in history. With respect to the dyadic-level analyses conducted previously, this suggests that the high levels of interdependence associated with conflictual relationships are less likely to obtain. Similarly, if we conceive of systemic interdependence as defined by major power relations, as Waltz emphasizes, then systemic interdependence and the conflict associated with it should be less likely. The expansion of globalization has created more linkages, which may have actually reduced the dangers that may be associated with depending too heavily on any one partner. Instead, states have the freedom to exit undesirable relationships. This suggests that the expansion of trade globally may be beneficial for peace, since it leads to less dependence at the dyadic level. At the same time, it is difficult to speak definitely about any of the propositions that would link major power trade to war. It is apparent that important trading partners may be allies or adversaries in war; similarly, adversaries may emerge from war and return to being important trading partners.[4] While globalization is expanding, in terms of the extent of types and extent of linkages between states around the globe, the amount that any one state is dependent upon another appears to be declining over time. Recent trends in globalization may have created freedoms that were not present in earlier historical periods that witnessed high economic interdependence. My analysis, however, does point to some exceptions to the apparent decline in dyadic dependence. In the case of China and Russia, we see each state relying more heavily on other major powers. The extent of dependence approaches the types of relationships that my findings suggest would reach dangerous levels of dependence.

Again, whether one considers the world more interdependent and more conflictual than in the past depends upon how we conceive of interdependence and conflict. What is apparent is that the growth of global trade may be associated with declines in partner dependence at the dyadic level, including dependence between major power dyads. In fact, the expansion of global trade offers new opportunities of freedom to redirect trade ties among a more diverse group of states. The dependence one has on any one state becomes less significant and perhaps less likely to engender conflict. In that respect, the decrease in dependence for the major powers may represent a positive development. Policy efforts to strengthen the bonds of dependence between these states may be met with caution. In the next chapter, I consider the policy implications of my findings in greater detail, particularly how they relate to dyadic interactions.

The analyses presented in this chapter reveal that where scholars focus their attention may alter the conclusion they reach about the impact of interdependence. The evidence suggests that some elements of trade may have a pacifying effect at the national level. Scholars should investigate more thoroughly the link between national and dyadic attributes of interdependent relationships. For example, I argue that trade's impact on conflict may vary depending upon the costs and benefits of a given relationship. Yet, I am assuming that some relationships are more costly or beneficial than others, without directly measuring whether this assumption is accurate. Unfortunately, it is difficult to measure the noneconomic benefits and costs of interdependence. I initially assumed that those states who were enjoying growth in GDP were more likely to derive benefits from trade and less likely to engage in conflict if they depend heavily on trade. In preliminary analyses (not reported here), I examined whether one-year and five-year growth patterns in total trade and/or GDP affected the basic analyses reported at the monadic level. I found no evidence that a state's enjoyment of positive growth in GDP or total trade reduced the likelihood that it would experience conflict. While I found this surprising, in light of my tendency to tie notions of growth in wealth to notions of trade's benefits, a more reasonable explanation for the lack of significance may reside in the tendency for wealthy states to engage in more conflicts. Even if some states are deterred from engaging in conflict during periods of relative growth, there appears to be a general tendency for wealthy states to have a greater propensity to engage in conflict. From this chapter, it also becomes clear that more work is needed to integrate theoretical propositions about the impact of trade on conflict at the monadic, dyadic, and system levels of analysis. Thus far, additional pieces of information about trading relationships appear to raise additional questions that require exploration.

Chapter 6

CONCLUSIONS

I began this study by posing a few simple questions concerning trade's impact on interstate relations, with the primary question being, Does trade promote peace? To address this question, I argued that it was necessary to investigate a more spatially and temporally diverse group of interstate relations than had previously been considered. In addition, I argued that it was necessary to go beyond the liberal portrayal of a commercial peace and consider alternative interpretations of the impact of trade on interstate relations. In turn, I surveyed the arguments advanced by an eclectic group of critics of liberal thought. Doing so enabled me to draw several conclusions about the overall influence of economic interdependence on interstate relations. In light of the empirical findings, I am now prepared to provide several responses to the questions advanced at the outset of this study.

GENERAL FINDINGS

The empirical analyses presented in this study provide little support for the argument that trade promotes peace in dyadic relationships. Instead, I find that interdependent dyads are more likely to engage in militarized conflicts than those with less extensive trade ties. While trade ties appear to aid states in achieving negotiated settlements to conflict, this enhanced negotiating capacity presumed to be associated with interdependence does not preclude the escalation of conflict. Rather, the evidence indicates that interdependent dyads are more likely to experience the most extreme form of conflict—war.

In turning to the state and system levels of analysis, I found that there are differences in trade's impact across different levels of analysis. In fact, there is some evidence that states that are heavily dependent on trade for their economy are less conflictual than others. However, we see that the economically strong states in the system are more conflictual than others, suggesting that there may be contradictions in the perceived dual policy goals of trade contributing to wealth and peace. Further investigation is needed to address the question of how my state-level findings relate to dyadic-level relationships. I assume that those states enjoying benefits from trade are the ones that are less likely to engage in conflict, but once again, it is difficult to translate monadic-level phenomena to dyadic-level analysis. Looking at the system level provided a less clear-cut picture about the possibilities for peace associated with increased interdependence. Depending upon how one conceives of both systemic interdependence and conflict, one's conclusions about the relationship may differ. The jury is still out on resolving this question, and further investigation is needed.

Does this mean that critics of liberalism are more accurate than the liberals in their predictions about trade's impact on conflict? In general, no one theoretical position provides an accurate account of the impact of trading relationships. The experience of states within trading relationships differs. As mentioned, few theorists explicitly articulate the hypothesized relationship between trade and conflict. Those that do so provide little explanation for factors that give rise to variations in trading relationships. Throughout this study, I have focused on one argument made by some critics of liberalism—that symmetrical dependence is different than asymmetrical dependence. From the relevant literature, I inferred that symmetrical ties may offer a hope for peace, since they offer states an opportunity to reap the benefits of trade without being subject to the political manipulation found in less symmetrical relationships. Asymmetrical relationships, on the other hand, subject less powerful states to adverse consequences that may nullify the deterrent effect of trade on conflict or may heighten tensions that make conflict more likely. In addition, symmetric ties should be more likely to confer relatively equal benefits to both partners, reducing the likelihood that conflicts will arise over the distribution of the gains for trade. Thus, I reasoned that the greatest hope for peace should arise in relations in which dependence was both symmetric and extensive.

However, the evidence does not support my initial proposition. *The pacifying effect of balanced dependence was seen only at the lowest level of trade ties.* Here, symmetric ties simply reflected the fact that states were relatively equal in their lack of dependence. That is, both states were relatively independent and were equal in that respect. On the other hand, *in situations of extensive trade dependence, states with symmetric ties were found to be more conflictual.* Thus, relationships that I expected to be the most peaceful were instead the most conflictual.

How might we explain this unanticipated finding? Why would the

conditions believed to promote peace be associated with the most frequent and intense conflicts? The answer may reside, in part, in explana-
tions emerging from beyond the economic interpretations of the trade-
conflict relationships. For example, we learn from sociological and
psychological theories that close relationships are more likely to exhibit
increased conflict and cooperation. Relations that exhibit both extensive
and mutual trade dependence may be more likely than others to witness
the establishment of additional forms of linkages. For example, when
dependence is asymmetric, the leader of the more powerful state may not
view the more dependent state as being an equal partner in the relationship and may be less likely to forge additional bonds beyond the economic realm. *Mutual need* in trade may motivate each state to strengthen
existing bonds in other areas. Thus, the web of interstate linkages may be
more extensive in relations among equal partners. And, it is this web of
interstate ties believed to foster peace that may contribute to the
increased propensity for conflict in interdependent relationships.

Interdependence, as some argue, may create more opportunities for
conflict to arise and more issues over which to conflict. Trade ties may
simply reflect the magnitude of other interactions between states. Yet,
interdependence does not reflect only quantitative differences in interactions; interdependent relations are assumed to be qualitatively different
from other types of relationships.

Most scholars recognize that all interdependent relationships entail
costly aspects. Foremost among these costs is the reduced ability of states
to pursue their own national objectives independent of external
influences. The policies and actions of one state may have an effect on its
other partners. Liberals advocate policy coordination as a means to
reduce the potentially adverse consequences of interdependence. Neo-
Marxists and neorealists, on the other hand, underscore the difficulties of
achieving policy coordination in interstate relations.

The inability of states to offset the costly aspects of dependence may
be the principal factor contributing to tension in trading relationships. If
policy coordination is one way to overcome this problem, the question
arises over which relationships are most conducive to achieving compromises that are likely to promote the common good. One could argue that
policy coordination is more difficult to achieve in asymmetrical relations,
since the more powerful actor possesses an advantaged bargaining position and may have no incentive to alter its domestic policies in order to

reduce the negative consequences of dependence for the weaker state. According to this view, relations between equal partners would be more conducive to achieving compromises in policy coordination. On the other hand, one could argue that in relationships between equal partners, each state is less likely to yield to the demands of its partner, which may result in stalemates, when negotiations over contested policies take place.

In discussing asymmetrical relations, I have highlighted the negative aspects of the coercive power afforded to the more powerful state. Yet, a powerful state's ability to impose its will on the weaker states may lead to more coordinated policies. Admittedly, such policies are more likely to favor the powerful state. Most people do not imagine relationships filled with coercion to constitute the types of harmonious trading relationships that liberals portray. Nevertheless, it seems plausible to argue that coercive power can be used to facilitate the rapid resolution of contentious policy issues. Unfortunately, policy disputes resolved through imposed demands (rather than negotiated outcomes) are likely to lead to greater long-term tensions. Thus, it remains unclear whether asymmetrical or symmetrical ties offer greater promise for producing coordinated policies that minimize the adverse consequences of dependence.

In general, leaders may view encroachment on a state's ability to determine its own policies, particularly in the domestic arena, to be a threat to national autonomy and even security. Historically, states tend to be unwilling to subordinate national interests for supranational objectives. Thus, the greatest hope for coordinated policies between interdependent states is likely to arise when there is a convergence of national and supranational objectives. Unfortunately, the liberal assumption that international trade immediately produces a convergence of state and global interests remains questionable.

Moreover, liberals argue that when conflicts of interest arise in interdependent relations, they will be resolved nonviolently. Beyond its empirical disconfirmation, the theoretical basis for this assertion is weak. Interdependent actors frequently engage in conflict. We know that intracommunity violence, family violence, and civil wars are common phenomena (more common than interstate conflict). In addition, enhanced mechanisms for conflict resolution do not appear to thwart violence. A cursory look at any newspaper will reveal the widespread use of violence by citizens of democratic states against their fellow citizens. At the same time, the citizens of these societies exhibit a great tendency to resort to conflict mediation or resolution through institutional and noninstitu-tional mechanisms (e.g., courts, therapists, mediators). Even when insti-tutional mechanisms exist to resolve conflicts within societies, violence persists. If anything, we must begin to question the very logic upon which the argument that greater integration promotes peace rests. Rather than be surprised that trade failed to promote peace in the evidence reviewed in this study, it appears more logical to have expected to see an increase in violence with the expansion of interdependence.

Given the overall findings, one may ask why the results presented here depart from other studies that reveal a negative relationship between trade and conflict. In part, differences arise over the phenomena scholars seek to explain. As mentioned at the onset, I focus on whether interde-pendence deters states from engaging in extreme forms of conflict behav-ior between states—militarized disputes. With few exceptions, related empirical studies that provide evidence that trade promote peace incor-porate cooperative and conflictual behaviors. Studies employing mea-sures of "net conflict" evaluate the overall dyadic relationship by looking at the number of cooperative events minus the number of conflictual events. Incorporating cooperative events, which are more numerous than the rare conflictual events examined in this study, means that coopera-tion outweighs conflict. Thus, the conclusion that trade promotes peace is based on the empirical finding that trading states experience more cooperation. This is, of course, an interesting finding, but it is one that does not exclude the possibility that trading states also conflict more than other states. It may merely support the contention that interdependent dyads experience more cooperation and more conflict than do other states.

Differences also arise in studies that focus exclusively on militarized conflicts. Several efforts to explore the sources of discrepant findings in empirical studies of the trade-conflict relationship have failed to identify one dominant factor as responsible for the variations (Barbieri 1996d, 1998). Among the many variations in research approaches, scholars dif-fer in the samples they analyze, the historical domain they explore, the manner in which they measure central concepts, and the choice of con-trol variables. If, as some suggest, trade has a universally pacifying effect on conflict, the evidence of this effect should hold up across different samples, historical domains, conditions established through the use of control variables, and dimensions of trade dependence captured in related measures. The findings presented here provide the most comprehensive assessment of liberalism's claim that economic ties inhibit the most extreme forms of conflict behavior. If there were a strong relationship between trade and peace, the evidence presented in this study should have pointed in that direction.

This study, while answering some questions, raises additional questions that require further exploration. At the outset, I argued that anecdotal evidence about the impact of trade fails to inform us about whether a systematic relationship exists between trade and conflict. Yet, having uncovered evidence of that systematic relationship, it is clear that the large-N quantitative analyses have their own limitations. While I employ measures designed to capture the variations in interdependent relationships that may account for the differing impact of trade ties, a more detailed examination of the dynamics within interdependent relationships is needed. Given the ambiguities presented in the literature relevant to the trade-conflict debate, further explanatory power and theoretical enrichment might come from supplementing large-N studies with detailed case study analyses. The latter approach would provide some of the details about the missing links in the puzzle about countervailing tendencies of economic interdependence.

POLICY IMPLICATIONS

The empirical analyses presented in the previous chapters have important policy implications for the post–Cold War era. Many scholars and policymakers increasingly credit trade with contributing to the post–World War II peace, arguing that the continued expansion of trade ties will produce a similar effect in the post–Cold War era. The findings of this study suggest a reevaluation of policies designed to foster extensive trade ties.

Rather than simply assuming that trade will always promote peace, policymakers must consider the nature and context of economic linkages. In addition, if policymakers are to begin to formulate policies more consistent with the goals of peace, they must begin to recognize the shortcomings of policies designed according to the unconditional liberal premise that trade will always promote peace. By understanding the factors most likely to inhibit conflict in trading relations, political leaders will be better equipped to assess the potential impact of interdependence and to identify those relationships that are most likely to maximize the benefits of economic relationships, while minimizing costs of economic relationships.

In a similar way, scholars are now reevaluating the universal claims about the pacific nature of democratic states and are beginning to question the utility of policies designed to promote democracy among all states. Several scholars claim that states in the process of democratizing may be more conflict-prone than other states (Mansfield and Snyder 1995), that democratization has no significant effect on conflict processes (Thompson and Tucker 1997; Enterline 1995), and that democratic reversion increases the likelihood of interstate conflict (Ward and Gleditsch 1998). The empirical findings presented here suggest that trade may also have a positive influence on the conflict propensity of dyadic relations or have no influence at all. It may, therefore, be important to consider whether the concessions granted to states in the interest of fostering trade ties are worth the potential costs, particularly when the desired outcome is unlikely to obtain. States may still pursue strategies of expanded trade, in the hopes of profiting from economic relationships. Yet, they should not adopt the mistaken belief that trade ties will produce peaceful relationships.

It is also important to consider the implications of my findings with respect to the pacifying influence of symmetry and the presumed conflictual nature of asymmetrical ties at low levels of salience. Currently, Western leaders have sought to incorporate newly independent states into the world economy in the hope of securing a peaceful and prosperous future. The newly independent states of the former Soviet Union provide fertile ground for the West's economic expansion. The present economic standing of many Eastern European states makes it difficult to speak of their relations with the West as symmetrically dependent. Rather, asymmetrical ties may create a vicious circle of dependence and potential contempt that mirrors that found in North-South relations in the post–World War II era. For many of the newly independent states in the post–World War II era, legal independence did not mean economic or political freedom. In addition, the legacy of neocolonialism produced a gap in the distribution of wealth within and between nations and left questions about the viability of a stable peace in North-South relations. Thus, the asymmetrical trading relationships now being created may not only fail to foster peace, but may ultimately prove to be conflict prone.

Certainly, the evolving global economy must be considered when assessing the potential impact of trading relations. As the sheer volume of international trade grows, the flexibility of trading states to redirect trade patterns increases. In many respects this may offer benefits for trading states and a greater potential to achieve peace through trade. One of the primary negative attributes of dependent relations resides in the inability of dependent states to redirect their trade patterns when faced with undesirable economic relationships. As the flexibility of trade linkages increases, the relationships that emerge may be more reflective of the liberal perception of beneficial trade. That is, when a relationship poses undesirable political or economic costs, states have more freedom to exit the relationship. Unfortunately, many of the structural vestiges of dependence created through colonialism and imperialism persist in North-South relations, limiting the freedom of less powerful states to diversify their trade patterns. As noted, a similar pattern of structural dependence may emerge between emerging economies and dominant states. While most would agree that autarky is not a viable option for developing states, it appears that other policy options must be explored that take into account a more realistic picture of the range of possibilities in the outcome of trading policies. People must consider the negative consequences of trade and interdependence if they are to understand better how to avoid some of the pitfalls of interdependence.

One further trend must be identified in anticipating the impact of trade relations in the post–Cold War era. Given the findings presented here, it appears that the tendency to promote regional trading blocs as a means to derive greater economic benefits may have detrimental political consequences. For the results here indicate that it is extensive trade ties, especially among mutually dependent states, that appear to have the most damaging impact on interstate relations. This is particularly true when trade partner concentration is high, as will presumably be the case in regional trading agreements. Although regional trading agreements signal a willingness of states to cooperate in pursuit of mutual benefits, nations are generally resolute in pursuing national priorities over supranational goals. Thus, uniting states in the intricate web of linkages found in interdependent relations may prove to have more costs than benefits. In addition, the prospect for conflict is much greater when states pursue extensive as opposed to minor ties; that is, trade with minimum dependence may be a sounder policy than complete interdependence.

One additional trend in economic relationships is important to consider—the changing structure of the global economy. The inability of states to respond to shifting demands in the global economy has heightened tensions over trading issues. In particular, the most powerful states no longer garner the same benefits from the world trading system that they once enjoyed. Leaders that are unable to adjust their economy to respond to the changing demands of the global marketplace may turn to scapegoating. Tensions over economic issues may increase as the stakes of economic policies become more critical. Slow economic growth, combined with tensions over trade imbalances, appears to have heightened hostilities over a host of trading issues. Perceptions that one state may be deriving disproportionate gains from trade have led to charges of unfair trading practices. In the past, concerns about relative gains may have been less pronounced since economic expansion enabled more states to derive greater gains from trade. However, the financial crises of the 1990s and the economic hardships these produced may heighten perceptions that the economic pie is shrinking. Whether economic growth is faltering or not, the perception of a shrinking pie, in itself, may create concerns over the distribution of that pie.

Clearly, my predictions paint a grim picture. My intent is not to argue that states should turn back the clock of global integration, but to stress the need to understand the potential impact of increased interdependence. Designing policies based on faulty assumptions about trade's impact benefits no one. If policymakers understand the potential impact of trade ties, they will be better equipped to find ways to stem the tide of tensions that may erupt in such relationships. Ideally, states will devise measures to minimize the costs associated with interdependence, while also maximizing its benefits. They must also consider the overall context in which trading relationships are embedded in evaluating whether it is desirable to expand dependence on any given state.

Possible Scenarios

Given the rarity of militarized disputes, the magnitude of the influence of interdependence on conflict (as of any one factor believed to affect militarized conflict) appears minor. Nevertheless, it is useful to consider the directional influence of interdependence on conflict and the relationships most likely to minimize the risk of conflict. To do this, it is helpful to consider a few possible scenarios that a leader might face in considering whether to increase trade ties with a particular partner.

Imagine that a leader of State A is evaluating its trading relationship with State B and is considering whether to increase its trade dependence on State B. Assume State A can only alter its own policies toward State B—it cannot influence State B's dependence on the relationship. Assume also that the leader of State A is concerned with maximizing security and seeks to alter its trade dependence in a manner consistent with minimizing the probability of getting into a militarized dispute. Even if the leader assumes that increased trade results in greater gains from trade, placing security concerns foremost on the agenda means that he or she will increase trade dependence only when it seems to offer an increased opportunity for peace. The benefits acquired from expanded trade will not offset the costs of greater insecurity.

Now, let us imagine three possible relationships that State A could have to its trade partner—State B. Recall from figure 1 that the Interdependence-Dependence Continuum consists of four quadrants. Quadrants I and IV represent asymmetrical trading relations; quadrants II and III represent symmetrical relations, with quadrant III representing minor linkages and quadrant II indicating extensive interdependence. Using the logit estimates from the analysis of MID occurrence for the period 1870–1992 that are reported in table 1, I calculate the dispute probabilities corresponding to different configurations of trade-partner dependence for a given dyad, Dyad$_{ab}$.

Figure 6 illustrates the dispute probabilities corresponding to the various configurations of trade dependence. The first figure, (a), depicts the lowest range of quadrant III, where each state conducts no more than 10 percent of its trade with a given partner. This scenario represents the most typical type of dyad in the sample, with 90 percent of observed cases in this study falling within this cell. Thus, this scenario is particularly interesting to consider. The next two cases, (b) asymmetrical and (c) symmetrical and highly salient relationships, are less typical, but worthy of consideration. The trend toward greater regional integration, as well as asymmetrical trading arrangements, may make these relationships more common in the post–Cold War era.

Imagine that State A can make only incremental changes in its trade dependence in the short term (i.e., moving outside the quadrant considered may provide alternative scenarios not considered here). In figure 6 (a), I find that the optimal position for maximizing security occurs at the lowest point of mutual dependence (0, 0). The probability of a dispute in a given year is 0.003 when no trade ties exist, compared to 0.008 at position (.1, .1). Regardless of State B's initial level of trade dependence

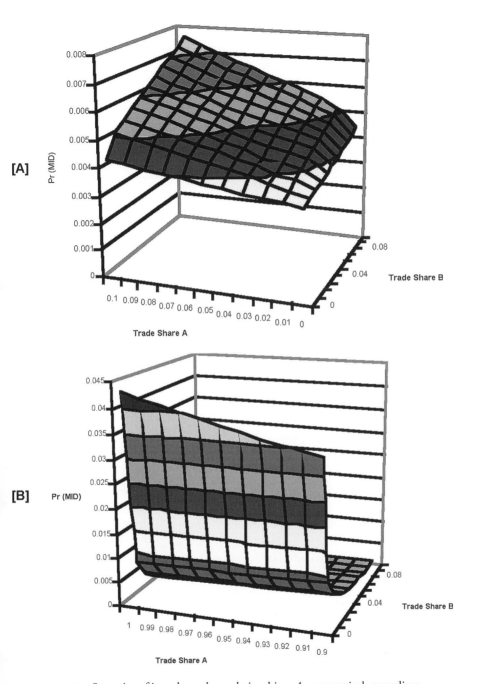

FIG. 6. Scenarios of interdependent relationships: *A,* symmetrical, nonsalient
relationships (quadrant III); *B,* asymmetrical relationships (quadrants I and IV);
C, symmetrical, salient relationships (quadrant II).

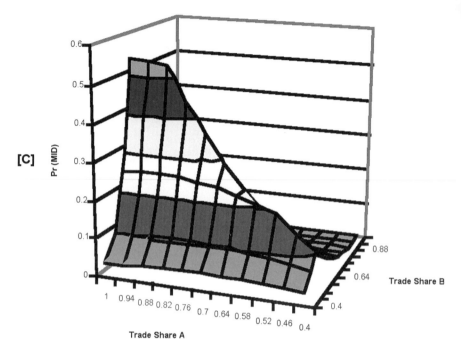

[C]

FIG. 6(C)

within this quadrant, State A will always be better off from a security maximization perspective in reducing its trade dependence on B. This leads to the conclusion that for the most typical type of trading relationship, leaders are better off minimizing trade dependence, if security maximization is a priority. In fact, it appears that this is the position that most states take with respect to trade. Whether intentional or not, in most cases states fail to depend on any one partner for more than 10 percent of their trade. In only about 10 percent of the cases observed in the sample do states exceed a dependence level of more than 10 percent with any one partner.

In figure 6 (b) I consider the case of an asymmetrical trading relationship. State A conducts between 90 and 100 percent of its trade with State B, while State B conducts no more than 10 percent of its total trade with State A. Cases such as these are observed in the sample, but are extremely rare. Less than 1 percent of the observations in this study represent cases where a state relies on one partner for more than 90 percent of their total trade. In such a situation, the optimal move for State A would depend on State B's position. If State B conducts less than 10 percent of its trade with State A, A is better off reducing its trade dependence on B. In this range of highly unequal dependence, the greater A's reduction in dependence, the lower the probability of conflict. On the other hand, within this quadrant, if State B conducts more than 10 percent of its trade with A, State A is better off increasing its trade dependence on State B. The optimal position for minimizing conflict actually occurs at the position (1, .1). The less dependent state (State B) is always better off increasing its trade dependence on A. This extreme form of asymmetrical relations makes each state less secure, which could be compensated by a move toward greater symmetry.

Figure 6(c) illustrates the case in which State A and State B have highly salient and symmetrical dependence, where each state conducts more than 40 percent of its trade with the other. This case represents an extremely atypical situation. The more typical scenarios are those where dyads are either symmetrical and nonsalient or else asymmetrical. In this relationship, a movement toward symmetry increases the likelihood of conflict. If State A's trade share is larger than State B's, State A is better off increasing its dependence on B. However, if State A's trade dependence is lower than State B, decreasing dependence is more desirable. If one state moves toward the region of greater symmetry, the other state should move to a position of relative asymmetry. We see that the impact of symmetry varies across different types of dyadic relationships. In the first scenario, symmetrical relations are more pacific, while here, they are more conflictual.

Finally, we may depart from the approach taken in the previous scenarios to consider a different perspective of viewing the trade-conflict relationship. If we adopt the liberal view that states are concerned with maximizing welfare, rather than security, the optimal policy would differ. A state might be willing to forfeit greater security for greater gains from trade. Perhaps the more realistic approach would be to recognize that states derive utility from both welfare and security. However, an increase in the gains from trade appears to require a trade-off with security.

If a leader's decision calculus incorporates concerns for maximizing welfare and security, then decisions to alter one's trade policy would depend upon a number of factors, including the utility a leader ascribed to welfare relative to security goals, the risk acceptance of a leader, and the nature of the trading relationship. Some leaders might be willing to forfeit the gains from trade associated with expanded trade ties in the interest of greater security (i.e., a reduced likelihood of experiencing a dispute). On the other hand, a leader might be willing to risk the higher likelihood of a dispute in the interest of acquiring greater gains from trade. Whether a leader substitutes gains from trade for security will, in part, depend upon the utility he or she assigns to security versus gains from trade. In addition, a leader's decision to substitute welfare for security will in part depend upon his or her propensity toward risk acceptant behavior. For example, if a leader recognizes the rarity of militarized disputes, he or she may incorporate a consideration of the probability of a dispute actually occurring into the decision calculus for expanding trade ties. Given the rarity of disputes, the probability of incurring the costs of conflict is lower than that of attaining the benefits of trade. Again, the nature of the relationship must also be considered, since there are instances where an increase in dependence requires no security trade-off. The primary point I hope to underscore from these scenarios is that trade decisions involve implicit costs to national security, a view at sharp variance with the traditional liberal approach. These costs must be evaluated relative to the benefits from trade when considering strategies for altering trade policies. Obviously, further attention must be devoted to assessing the factors that might influence a leader's decision calculus, yet this approach may offer a more realistic assessment of the trade-conflict relationship than that provided by alternative models.

THE FUTURE

This study stimulates some important issues for future research. Perhaps the primary component missing from this and related research would be a more adequate assessment of the costs and benefits incurred through interdependence. I have repeatedly argued that the conflictual or pacific elements of interdependence are directly related to perceptions about trade's costs and benefits. Yet, a more comprehensive evaluation of these costs and benefits is needed to see whether a link truly exists between the benefits enjoyed in a given trading relationship and the inhibition of conflict in that relationship or, conversely, the presence of net costs for at least one trading partner and the presence of conflict in that relationship.

For example, we should consider whether trading relationships that contain two partners believed to benefit from trade are more pacific than those relationships that contain at least one state believed to be worse off from trade. In this study I have merely outlined the types of relationships believed to confer the greatest benefits, but such benefits and costs require more rigorous investigation.

In addition, while liberals generally assume benefits increase with the expansion of trade, benefits may actually conform to the law of diminishing returns. Costs, on the other hand, may grow exponentially, as interdependence grows. Thus, if we evaluate the net benefits of interdependence, costs may outweigh benefits as interdependence increases. Again, further investigation is necessary to evaluate the functional form consistent with the rise and/or decline of costs and benefits in interdependent relations. Of course, assessing the political costs of interdependence may be more difficult than assessing the economic benefits. For example, it is easier to evaluate the variations in national growth corresponding to greater participation in trade than to assess the political impact of dependence, such as losses in national autonomy.

Another area that requires further consideration concerns the interactive effects of several types of interdependence for fostering interstate peace. One of the primary components of liberal theory focuses on the convergence of interests and the transmission of commonalties that arise through economic and noneconomic linkages. While I have controlled for several types of interstate bonds, further attention is needed to uncover the combined effect of expanding interstate bonds in multiple areas. There may be countervailing influences from different forms of interstate interdependence.

Throughout this study I have underscored the two dominant perceptions about interstate linkages, one suggesting that greater ties foster peace, the other suggesting that interdependence increases the likelihood of conflict. Empirical evidence suggests that different forms of interdependence may have different effects on conflict. For example, contiguity is consistently found to increase the likelihood of conflict, while the commonalties believed to be associated with joint democracy are generally found to inhibit conflict. Scholars tend to focus on the same notion of interstate ties to explain both the pacific and conflictual nature of these two types of interstate ties. In fact, some of the same theorists who argue that the high levels of contact associated with contiguity give rise to conflict suggest that the ties promoted through joint democracy will give rise to peace. We can only conclude that interstate ties foster both peace and conflict. Yet, we need to determine why greater ties in one area may be more conducive for peace, while in other areas, interdependence will increase conflict. Again, we are left with the conclusion that it is not interdependence itself, but some element of that relationship, that gives rise to variations in its impact on conflict.

Although part of the answer may reside in the costs and benefits of interdependent relationships and the manner in which this influences conflict decisions, it is clear that the dynamics described in psychological and sociological theories of close relationships may have important implications for studies of interstate interdependence. For instance, these theories may help uncover the mystery of the factors that tip the balance between conflict and cooperation that clearly coexist among interdependent actors. Exploring this question has implications for trading relations, as well as other forms of relations between actors in world politics.

In a similar vein, further investigation is required in order to understand the interrelationship between conflict and cooperation in interdependent relations. This is particularly true among states whose destinies may be linked, but where the link is established through conflictual interactions (e.g., enduring rivalries). As in other dyadic relationships, it is important to understand how the promotion of cooperation may dampen conflictual behaviors. Similarly, it is necessary to consider the simultaneous influences of trade and conflict. Here, I considered only the influence of interdependence on conflict, but, as discussed previously, conflict likely affects interdependence. However, a more complete assessment of the factors influencing trade patterns may be needed to evaluate the influence of trade on conflict, and that of political factors on trade.

In addition, recent discussions over the most appropriate measures of interdependence tended to view GDP- and total trade–based measures as alternative methods of operationalizing the same phenomena. As discussed, these measures may actually be capturing related, but distinct, dimensions of interdependence. Further tests are needed to evaluate why some forms of dependence produce different results on interstate relations. In addition, researchers are exploring new ways to capture the importance of commodities in evaluating trade dependence. Obviously, dependence and interdependence captures myriad interstate ties, some of which remain unexplored or unoperationalizable.

Finally, one missing link in the trade-conflict relationship resides in the nexus of domestic politics and international relations. Generally, political economists and others focus on the internal conditions and domestic coalitions influencing trade policies (Rogowski 1989). On the other hand, this study and related studies of interdependence focus on the relationship between states, with little attention devoted to the internal forces influencing trade policies. As in the case of assessing costs and benefits, it would be useful to consider how the realization of costs and benefits among different domestic political and economic coalitions influences trading relationships, which may then influence the expected utility of trade and conflict (Brawley 1993; Rosecrance and Stein 1993). The applicability of two-level games to the trade-conflict relationship remains the most unexplored avenue for future research (Putnam 1988).

While I sought to answer several questions about the trade-conflict relationship, it should be quite obvious that interdependence—both as a concept and a relationship—is more complex than generally thought. It is also clear that economic ties have a significant influence on conflict. Most observers realize that economic relationships matter; my analyses have specified how they matter. Although my findings indicate that the impact of interdependence on conflict is not akin to the vision espoused by liberals, the tendency for conflict researchers to exclude this important relationship can no longer be justified. We see that economic interdependence does affect interstate relations—and not in the ways predicted by those who believe trade promotes peace.

As in any vibrant field, there will be disagreements, struggles, and eventually advancement. I do not view what I have written here as the last word. Rather it is a very modest start—it is an attempt to rethink conventional thinking in a way that will in the long run advance the field. Social science is a messy process, but when the dust settles we usually see progress. My fondest hope is that what I have written will prompt others to take pen in hand and modify and improve the ideas and claims advanced in these pages. It is only through such back-and-forth progress that we can begin to understand more fully the complicated workings of trade on the international system.

Appendix A

NOTES ON TRADE DATA

The trade database project began in 1991 as part of my doctoral research, but remains ongoing. The International Trade Database employed in this analysis is a revised and expanded version of the database described and employed in my dissertation research (Barbieri 1995). The database includes dyadic trade-flow figures and national import and export figures. These data are available at the Peace Science Society (International) website at <http://pss.la.psu.edu/intsys.htm>.

OVERVIEW OF DATABASE PROJECT

Data were collected for all sovereign states within the interstate system, as defined by the Correlates of War (COW) Project for the period 1870–1992. Few observations are available for the years corresponding to World War I and World War II.[1] Those that were available are included in the analyses.[2] The data set only includes reported statistics derived from trade reports; no estimation techniques were employed to replace missing values, as discussed later.

Missing data for exchange rates, cases including only partial information about dyadic flows or national totals, and reports containing unrealistic values are coded as missing values. Unrealistic values include those cases where dyadic trade exceeds the total trade of one of the nations in the dyad. This situation can arise from a number of factors including erroneous trade reports, inconsistencies between partner reports, and dramatic fluctuations in the exchange rates that are applied to the trade figures (e.g., national totals may be reported in USD, while dyadic figures were transformed with exchange rates that can vary widely from one year to the next).

COLLECTION PROCEDURES AND
ENTERING DATA

Stuart Bremer designed a program to generate all possible combinations of dyads within the interstate system for a given year. This was used to construct annual databases to enter the trade data. In all cases, trade figures are reported only when they were available for the given year cor-

139

responding to the matrix; no interpolation or extrapolation techniques were used. For example, if China's trade is absent in 1899, but present for 1898 and 1900, I did not interpolate the figures to derive a figure for 1899, but counted that point as missing data. My rationale for refraining from interpolation and extrapolation techniques resides in my belief that many historical reports already include cases where states or publishers have employed these techniques to replace missing values. Additional data manipulation would introduce further error by assuming that trade conformed to a particular trend, when missing data may instead correspond to periods in which real changes in trade patterns took place. In addition, the absence of trade figures may represent a genuine cessation of trading relations. Since it is impossible to distinguish missing information from absent flows, no values for missing data were assumed.

Special trade of commodities, rather than general trade, is reported. *Special trade* entails imports for home consumption and exports of domestically produced goods, while *general trade* includes transit trade. In most cases states report separate categories for special and general trade. However, in some cases states fail to distinguish between special and general trade or only report general trade.

Trade with colonies is excluded from dyadic transactions and national totals for states possessing colonial territories. Although it would be interesting to include an analysis of trade between colonies and colonial powers, the limitations posed by unavailable data proved too great a hindrance to this goal.

In general, data reported by the importing nation are used for dyadic trade-flow figures. However, the scarcity of trade data prior to 1900 often required me to rely on one nation's accounts for both import and export figures. Since systematic reporting appears to be correlated with level of development, particularly in the nineteenth century, for the years preceding 1885 data were entered for both imports and exports by nation, according to an approximation of their level of development. That is, the data of developed states were entered first and supplemented by that provided by less developed states. Data entry for this period began with the major powers and was then supplemented by minor powers.

Checks for the accuracy of reports for the nineteenth century were conducted by examining the correlation of trade reports between trading partners. When one nation consistently reported figures similar to those reported by its partners, the state was deemed to be a credible source.

When a discrepancy arose between trading partners, I relied on the reports of the state that consistently reported flows similar to those reported by the majority of its partners (i.e., where matched partner reports were more consistent). Figures for states that consistently overvalued or undervalued their dyadic flows were scrutinized when a drastic discrepancy in reports occurred. Here, again, the dyadic flow reported by the more reliable reporting state was used.

After 1900, and particularly after 1910, data are more readily available for all independent states. From 1900 through 1945 data were first recorded by the figures reported by the importing nation. When entering data into the trade matrix in a given year, I proceeded through the matrix by country, entering all reported import values with each trading partner. After completing all states' records of imports, I proceed through the matrix once again by country and supplemented the missing data of dyadic flows with the information provided by exporting states. Again, it was necessary at times to rely on one state for both the import and export values within a dyadic relationship. However, this was avoided whenever possible.

The figures provided by the importing nation are used for several reasons. First, relying on either the importers' or exporters' reports permits me to utilize information derived from each state in a given dyad. This diminishes the error introduced if one state has a tendency to underreport or overreport its trade flows. Second, import figures were chosen rather than export figures, since they are generally considered more reliable and comprehensive than export records. The greater tendency for states to impose tariffs on imported rather than exported goods is believed to result in more rigorous efforts to adopt systematic measures to record import trade. Finally, relying on either import or export flows reduces the discrepancy of flows reported in c.i.f. (i.e., cost, insurance, freight or charged in full) and f.o.b. (i.e., free on board). The former includes costs of transferring the good to the point of consumption, while the latter excludes such costs. Imports are generally reported c.i.f. and exports f.o.b. Therefore, some variation in the importer and exporter's reports are expected. For example, the International Monetary Fund (1991) estimates that figures for c.i.f. are 10 percent greater than those reported in f.o.b. Relying on either the export or import flow will improve the consistency in the range of values reported by each state for one particular flow.

Aggregated Data

One difficulty imposed in the project resides in the problem of aggregated trade figures. In some instances a country combines the value of its trade with two or more nations. However, when trade with two or more states is explicitly identified, it is possible to use a triangular method to disaggregate trade flows. For example, if Great Britain combines the value of trade conducted with Spain and Portugal into one total, I examined the value that Spain and Portugal report as trading with Britain. When only one of these states reports its trade with Britain, the total of the reporting state was subtracted from the aggregated value provided in Britain's trade report. Thus, information was available for Britain's trade with two of its partners, by combining information provided by a third party.

Unfortunately, in both the pre– and post–World War II period, it is impossible to disaggregate the figures for the economic union of Belgium and Luxembourg. Both the League of Nations and the IMF provide the aggregated figure for the union. For the pre–World War II period trade statistics for the union are entered as Belgian trade, since Luxembourg accounts for a less significant share of the union's trade. This issue undoubtedly requires further attention in future research. For example, it may be possible to estimate the share of the union's trade conducted by Luxembourg in order to include Luxembourg into the analysis. At this time, little information was found to resolve this problem.

Another case of aggregated trade figures is more problematic and remains unresolved. In both the pre–World War II and post–World War II periods, national trade statistics generally include a category entitled "Trade with Other Countries" in which the values of transactions with minor trading partners are aggregated, but no list of states contained in this category is provided. It is therefore impossible to distinguish nations that possess no trade ties from those who possess minor trade flows. Some studies assume that the absence of a state's name from another nation's trade records denotes the absence of trade. Trade might actually exist, but be too minimal to include as a separate entry in the trade report. Since there are theoretical and methodological distinctions between zero trade and minor trade, missing data are treated as such, without substituting zero trade for absent trade figures. Clearly, the prospect for conflict to arise between states that have no ties whatsoever is significantly different from that which would exist between states that have some contact. Minor ties presuppose a relationship between states, while zero trade may indicate the absence of interstate interactions.

Currency Conversion

Most data were collected in local currency and converted to current U.S. dollars. The majority of exchange rates used for conversions were taken from the *Polity II* project (Gurr, Jaggers, and Moore 1989). The exchange rates listed in *Polity II* were originally collected by the Correlates of War Project, although some revisions were made by Gurr to account for dramatic discontinuities revealed in the time trends of individual exchange rates.[3] Several problems arose when converting trade figures from local currencies to U.S. dollars. The primary problem was the lack of available exchange rates for many states. In many instances trade data reports were available, but exchange rates were unavailable. In addition, *Polity II* contains a variable that lists the name of the national currency to which the exchange rate is presumed to correspond. However, in many instances no currency name is given.

According to the compilers of the data, when no name is given, the exchange rates should correspond to the national currencies reported in the *Statesman's Yearbook*. Yet, in some cases with a missing currency name, the state in question has multiple currencies. Thus, it was necessary to compile figures for exchange rates for many countries. (The problems encountered in the exchange rate project were as extensive as those confronted with the trade data, but are only described briefly here.) Upon further investigation, I found that some of the exchange rates reported in *Polity II* differed significantly from those found in two or more alternative sources.

Also, in some instances, particularly in Latin American states, the value of import and export flows are reported in two different currencies. For example, silver pesos may be used for imports, while gold pesos are used for exports. This requires separate exchange rates for converting imports and exports into U.S. dollar values.

A comprehensive assessment of exchange rates was undertaken, and data were compiled to supplement missing and questionable exchange rate values. Data for each nation's exchange rate series were reviewed to identify dramatic departures from the general time-series trend. These inconsistencies were investigated by reading country profiles to determine whether the nation experienced a change in currency or whether there were real variations attributable to hyperinflation or other trends. Wherever possible, multiple sources of exchange rates were compared to determine whether the values reported across sources were similar. In most cases, two reports were similar in value.

Sources for exchange rates include Bidwell (1970), *Currency Conversion Tables: A Hundred Years of Change* (London: Rex Collings); the *Statesman's Yearbook* (1870–1940); and U.S. Department of Commerce (1920–39), *Foreign Commerce Yearbook*. When using the *Statesman's Yearbook* as a source of exchange rates, conversions were first made from local currency to British pounds and then converted from pounds to dollars, since this source reports local currency in terms of British pounds.

Pre–World War II Trade Data

To acquire nineteenth- and early-twentieth-century trade data, an exhaustive search of historical documents, including national almanacs, commerce dictionaries, and government documents, was undertaken. Initially, I sought to collect data dating back to 1816, to correspond with what most international relations scholars identify as the beginning of the current interstate system. However, trade data for the pre-1870 period are too scarce to make any meaningful analysis possible. Thus, the project begins with the years following the unification of Germany and Italy.

The Statesman's Yearbook (1870–1940) was the primary source for trade figures for years preceding 1912. All volumes of the yearbook were used, since the trade figures for different countries do not always correspond with the almanac's publication dates. For example, the 1900 edition of *The Statesman's Yearbook* may contain values for China's trade for 1885 through 1887, but contain figures for the United States from 1898 through 1900. *The Statesman's Yearbook* contains country profiles that usually include tables of foreign trade figures. When these tables are not present, information was pieced together by reading entries related to a particular state's economic activities. For example, sections on economic activities may contain information about the country's total trade figures. In addition, references are often made to the share of trade conducted with a state's top trading partners. For example, an entry might explain that a third of the state's trade is conducted with a given partner. This information was used to derive the relevant dyadic trade figures from the total trade values. For the nineteenth century, many of the trade figures for developing states were obtained by this method.

Reviewing each country's economic profile was a tedious process, but it proved valuable for providing additional information about deviations from the general norms of national reports. For example, reading the country profile often identified information about multiple currencies operating within a given state or about revaluation of a currency.

Data for developing states are more readily available in tabular form after 1885. For the period 1873–85 U.S. Congressional records proved to be a useful source of trade data, in particular *U.S. Congress (House) Miscellaneous Documents* (1887), "Abstract of the Foreign Commerce of Europe, Australia, Asia and Africa, 1873–1885," United States Consular Reports, No. 85, October (Washington, DC: Government Printing Office). Data for this period were supplemented with other sources, including the *Statesman's Yearbook;* Mitchell (1982), *International Historical Statistics for Africa and Asia* (New York: New York University Press); Mitchell (1983), *International Historical Statistics for the Americas and Australasia* (Detroit: Gale); and Wattenberg (1976), *Introduction and User's Guide to The Statistical History of the United States from Colonial Times to the Present* (New York: Basic Books).

For the period 1912–1938, the primary source used was the League of Nations (1912–1945) annual publications of *International Trade Statistics* (Geneva: League of Nations). The title for this annual publication varies and includes *Memorandum on International Trade and the Balance of Payments and International Trade Statistics.* Data were taken from each annual volume. In addition, some data for 1935 and 1938 were derived from the League of Nations (1942), *The Review of World Trade.* League of Nations' data were supplemented with data from *The Statesman's Yearbook* and Mitchell (1982, 1983).

Post–World War II Trade Data

For the post–World War II period, the majority of trade data are derived from the International Monetary Fund's (Inter-university Consortium for Political and Social Research, 1991) *Direction of Trade Statistics electronic tape.* Data were reconfigured from national accounts to dyadic trade flows. As in the pre–World War II case, reports of dyadic trade flows were derived from the importing countries' reported trade figures.

When these figures were absent, the exporter's reports were used. The values that each state reports to import from each partner were added to derive the dyadic total. Each state's total imports and export figures were combined to arrive at each nation's total trade.

In many instances, the electronic version of the IMF data tape reports trade flows as zero or missing, but these trade values are reported in their annual publications. Missing data were investigated and supplemented with the International Monetary Fund's *International Financial Statistics* (Washington, DC: IMF Statistics Department, Monthly 1956–98) and *The Direction of Trade Statistics Yearbook* (Washington, DC: Real Sector Division, IMF Statistics Department, Quarterly 1956–98). Missing data for the post–World War II period have not all been investigated. This project remains ongoing.

Other sources for the post–World War II period include Arthur S. Banks (1979), *Cross-National Time-Series Data Archive* (Binghamton, NY: Center for Social Analysis); The United Nations *Yearbook of International Trade Statistics,* later renamed *International Trade Statistics Yearbook* (New York: Department of International Economic and Social Affairs Statistical Office, Annual 1950–96); Europa Publications, *The Europa Year Book,* vol. 1, *Europe* (London: Europa, Annual 1960–96); M. C. Kaser and E. A. Radice, eds. (1985), *The Economic History of Eastern Europe, 1919–1975,* vol. 1, *Economic Structure and Performance between the Two Wars* (Oxford: Clarendon); Paul Maher (1972), *Soviet and East European Foreign Trade, 1946–1969* (Bloomington: Indiana University Press); State Statistical Bureau of the People's Republic of China, Renze Zhang, ed., *China Statistical Yearbook* (New York: Praeger, 1990); Wray O. Candilis (1968), *The Economy of Greece, 1944–66.* (New York: Praeger). Rodger A. Clarke and Dubravko J. I. Matko (1983), *Soviet Economic Facts, 1917–1981* (New York: St. Martin's); Zbigniew M. Fallenbuchl, ed. (1976), *Economic Development in the Soviet Union and Eastern Europe,* vol. 2 (New York: Praeger); David Lascelles (1976), *Comecon to 1980* (London: Financial Times); Marie Lavigne, ed. (1990), *The Soviet Union and Eastern Europe in the Global Economy* (Cambridge: Cambridge University Press); V. P. Gruzinov (1979), *The USSR's Management of Foreign Trade* (White Plains, NY: M. E. Sharpe); John B. Quigley (1974), *The Soviet Foreign Trade Monopoly* (Columbus: Ohio State University Press); William Nelson Turpin (1977) *Soviet Foreign Trade, Purpose and Performance* (Lexington, MA:

Lexington Books); U.S. Department of Commerce, various publications including *Selected U.S.S.R. and Eastern European Trade and Economic Data* (Bureau of East-West Trade, May 1974); *Selected U.S.S.R. and Eastern European and Economic Data* (Bureau of East-West Trade, June 1973); *Selected Trade and Economic Data of the Centrally Planned Economies* (Bureau of East-West Trade, May 1975); *The Chinese Economy and Foreign Trade Perspective—1976* (Bureau of East-West Trade, June 1977).[4]

Coding Rules for Trade Data

In my early research I treated zero and missing values as missing data. I now generally include zero values only if these values have been investigated and multiple sources have revealed little or no trade between states. Differences in coding rules for dealing with missing data can lead to significant variations in trade data sets among researchers, particularly since missing data account for such a large percentage of overall dyadic trade figures. Some researchers treat missing values as zero values, but I would caution researchers about adopting this rule. In some cases, data for country trade totals are missing, even if there is evidence that the state engages in trade. Thus, one cannot assume that a missing datum implies no trade. As mentioned previously, I have found the same tendency with the zero values reported by the IMF, where zero values may simply mean missing values.

In discussions with other scholars collecting or employing trade data, I found a number of areas in which scholars differ on decision rules regarding trade figures. This may be the source of discrepant empirical findings on issues such as trade and conflict, where different coding decisions lead scholars to assign different values to the degree of trade between states. Scholars employing trade data should think through the decision rules they adopt and consider how these rules might alter empirical findings. This is an area of research that requires further investigation.

Appendix B

MAJOR POWER TRADE

TABLE B1. AUSTRIA-HUNGARY'S TRADE WITH MAJOR POWERS

	France	Germany	Italy	Japan	Russia	UK	U.S.
1871			6.60		1.85	1.60	
1875	1.52		6.86		2.91	1.13	
1880	5.54	30.99	12.61		6.99	1.85	
1885	4.88	31.87	13.07		6.22	2.87	
1890		43.14	8.26	0.06	4.94	5.19	2.42
1895	5.85	32.0[a]	11.62	0.13	7.29	4.77	3.34
1900	6.73	40.5[b]	14.37	0.65	8.84	5.09	4.62
1905	3.19	38.47	6.70		4.27	4.41	6.20
1910	3.68	38.35	7.61	0.18	4.75	7.71	6.01
1913	2.58	37.02	7.46	0.2[c]	4.15	4.68	3.34

[a]1896 figure used for trade with Germany.
[b]1901 figure used for trade with Germany.
[c]1912 figure used for trade with Japan.

TABLE B2.   FRANCE'S TRADE WITH MAJOR POWERS

Pre–World War I

	Austria-Hungary	Germany	Italy	Japan	UK	U.S.	Russia
1870		3.65	7.75		25.24	7.62	3.23
1875	0.91	9.89	8.19	1.17	16.89	5.94	3.20
1880	1.80	9.42	6.82	0.33	21.93	12.51	4.09
1885	1.76	9.40	6.13	0.45	17.78	7.28	2.45
1890		8.46	3.32	0.77	18.91	9.84	2.95
1895	1.34	9.51	3.68	1.68	22.80	8.51	3.76
1900	1.50	10.13	3.46	0.79	21.39	9.16	3.55
1905	1.19	8.00	3.05	0.68	15.68	8.67	2.77
1910	1.51	10.62	4.02	0.94	14.86	8.51	3.58
1913	1.08	11.67	3.40	0.98	14.10	10.55	3.98

Interwar Period

	Germany	Italy	Japan	Russia	UK	U.S.
1920	4.59	3.13	0.79	0.35	19.88	17.79
1925	4.71	4.16	0.68	0.29	16.61	10.88
1931[a]	12.24	3.49	0.49	0.95	11.76	8.01
1935	7.77	2.73	0.79	1.69	8.52	7.32
1938	6.73	1.36	0.68	1.18	9.14	9.37

Post–World War II

	China	Russia	UK	U.S.
1950			7.68	9.43
1955		1.01	6.47	7.74
1960		1.60	4.62	9.00
1965	0.02		5.20	8.64
1970	0.03		4.99	7.80
1975	0.51		5.77	5.96
1980	0.31	2.40	6.47	6.49
1985	0.58	2.17	8.28	8.63
1990	0.86	1.11	8.36	7.22
1992	1.05	1.23	8.35	7.41

[a]1931 figures are used, since they are more complete than 1930 figures.

TABLE B3.   GERMANY'S TRADE WITH MAJOR POWERS

Pre–World War I

	Austria-Hungary	France	Italy	Japan	Russia	UK	U.S.
1870		4.19	0.33		14.82	21.22	6.96
1875		15.04	0.90	0.07	20.68		7.65
1880	12.13	11.36	2.04		9.62	14.82	6.50
1885	11.51	9.42	3.15	0.15	8.42	13.89	4.74
1890	12.36	7.39	3.06	0.42	9.74	12.21	10.91
1895	11.41	6.84	2.99	0.69	9.99	12.73	10.46
1900	13.40	6.72	2.91	0.63	10.08	11.42	11.56
1905	11.16	6.25	3.47	0.78	11.65	11.33	12.06
1910	9.94	6.72	3.98	0.73	13.32	11.67	10.69
1913	9.26	6.96	3.87	1.37	13.54	11.78	11.92

Interwar Period

	France	Italy	Japan	Russia	UK	U.S.
1920	11.49	4.49	0.69		13.45	26.17
1925	3.91	4.12	1.08	2.16	8.91	13.61
1931	8.97	3.52	1.03	7.13	10.08	6.69
1935	5.55	5.73	1.33	2.95	7.27	5.20
1938	3.38	5.41	1.35	0.75	5.79	5.16

TABLE B4. ITALY'S TRADE WITH MAJOR POWERS

Pre–World War I

	Austria-Hungary	France	Germany	Japan	UK	U.S.	Russia
1870	18.1[a]	29.19	1.09		21.57	4.48	3.50
1875	19.02	37.93	2.74		14.37	3.23	3.36
1880	14.76	24.58	6.11		9.42	5.53	4.39
1885	12.47	16.24	8.33		8.88	4.36	4.05
1890	10.28	12.60	13.29	0.08	12.68	10.56	5.89
1895	8.66	11.97	13.53	0.74	10.51	10.23	5.62
1900	9.25	10.03	12.67	0.64	10.26	10.29	4.76
1905	8.13	9.97	14.52	0.49	11.40	11.81	6.04
1910	8.06	10.40	16.28	0.56	12.08	11.47	5.83
1913	7.89	8.57	16.39	1.06	12.70	13.22	4.59

Interwar Period

	France	Germany	Japan	Russia	UK	U.S.
1920	10.57	6.06	0.89	0.27	17.32	28.10
1925	9.87	11.77	0.27	1.2[b]	10.30	18.16
1931	8.71	12.01	0.36	3.91	11.20	11.60
1935	6.12	18.00	0.46	1.86	7.61	10.39
1938	2.65	20.92	0.35	0.5[c]	6.18	9.80

[a]1871 figure used for trade with Austria-Hungary.
[b]1926 figure used for trade with Russia
[c]1937 figure used for trade with Russia.

TABLE B5. JAPAN'S TRADE WITH MAJOR POWERS

Pre–World War I

	Austria-Hungary	France	Germany	Italy	Russia	UK	U.S.
1870						19.40	8.56
1875		20.5[a]	1.84			29.21	21.15
1880		14.9[b]	1.75			28.38	27.51
1885		9.62	3.29			19.22	23.08
1890	0.24	8.89	5.60	0.25	0.51	18.25	17.4[c]
1895	0.17	9.89	5.67	1.35	1.13	12.65	14.88
1900	0.95	5.21	6.26	1.45	0.18	21.59	15.14
1905[d]	0.45	5.17	5.81	1.42	1.37	14.14	22.36
1910	0.43	5.45	6.68	1.26	0.57	14.93	23.11
1913	0.4[e]	4.28	10.04	1.84	0.62	17.87	29.71

Interwar Period

	France	Germany	Italy	Russia	UK	U.S.
1920	1.68	0.58	0.55	0.18	10.93	39.59
1925	1.29	2.46	0.21	0.33	4.97	28.93
1931	0.89	2.56	0.27	1.52	3.95	23.97
1938	0.92	3.62	0.25	0.31	3.81	24.20

[a]1876 figure used for trade with France.
[b]1881 figure used for trade with France.
[c]1891 figure used for trade with the US.
[d]1906 figures used.
[e]1912 figure used for trade with Austria-Hungary.

TABLE B6.   Russia's Trade with Major Powers

Pre–World War I

	Austria-Hungary	France	Germany	Italy	Japan	UK	U.S.
1870		9.09	36.25	2.61		42.79	1.00
1875	4.86	8.93	37.96	2.03		21.85	
1880	5.37	9.69	18.87	2.88		16.81	
1885	5.56	6.08	20.85	3.79		19.12	
1890	4.41	8.02	30.33	4.23	0.12	24.73	1.69
1895	3.47	7.83	28.91	3.59	0.40	24.58	1.75
1900	4.22	7.63	32.63	3.53	0.06	20.58	1.95
1905	4.71	8.23	44.30	5.49	0.6[a]	26.47	4.20
1910	4.30	7.92	46.51	4.99	0.22	24.55	4.08
1913	3.49	7.96	45.46	3.64	0.28	18.74	4.25

Interwar Period

	France	Germany	Italy	Japan	UK	U.S.
1925	1.85	16.64	2.86	1.11	16.19	11.98
1931	2.76	28.17	4.54	2.42	18.00	13.32
1935	7.65	18.66	3.73	2.80	25.00	8.02
1938	4.70	5.97		0.90	22.42	18.26

Post–World War II

	China	France	UK	U.S.
1950	22.49			
1955	40.93	1.36	3.90	0.29
1960	31.04	1.87	3.28	0.58
1965	5.53			
1970	0.52			
1975	0.40			
1980	0.34	4.15	1.40	1.38
1985	2.47	5.23	1.94	3.56
1990	4.24	4.76	2.62	4.33
1992	7.29	6.22	2.40	5.34

[a]1906 figure used for trade with Japan.

TABLE B7.   THE UNITED KINGDOM'S TRADE WITH
MAJOR POWERS

Pre–World War I

	Austria-Hungary	France	Germany	Italy	Japan	Russia	U.S.
1870	0.6[a]	11.81	8.64	2.68	0.37	7.12	16.15
1875	0.56	14.05	7.2[b]	2.58	0.64	6.51	20.70
1880	0.33	12.24	6.86	1.46	0.63	3.97	22.84
1885	0.46	7.89	6.14	1.49	0.40	3.42	17.04
1890	0.81	8.96	6.62	1.58	0.75	4.31	18.88
1895	0.62	12.86	9.97	1.82	1.21	6.65	25.45
1900	0.64	12.06	9.70	2.00	1.85	5.40	27.61
1905	1.22	11.70	10.83	2.60	2.11	6.65	24.23
1910	1.92	9.03	11.21	2.84	1.57	6.75	19.34
1913	0.99	7.13	9.99	2.55	2.06	4.73	15.66

Interwar Period

	France	Germany	Italy	Japan	Russia	U.S.
1920	6.71	1.82	1.73	1.75		21.31
1925	7.41	4.78	1.94	1.17	1.13	15.46
1931	5.81	6.79	2.22	1.07	3.07	10.55
1935	3.75	4.47	1.49	1.15	2.44	10.11
1938	3.12	3.95	1.09	0.96	1.93	10.34

Post–World War II

	China	France	Russia	U.S.
1950		3.21		7.26
1955		3.11	1.39	10.16
1960		2.63	1.60	11.73
1965		3.60		11.62
1970		4.52		12.55
1975	0.31	6.26		9.40
1980	0.40	7.19	0.90	10.77
1985	0.55	8.27	0.80	13.48
1990	0.59	9.23	0.68	11.26
1992	0.65	9.70	0.55	10.94

[a]1871 figure used for trade with Austria-Hungary.
[b]1876 figure used for trade with Germany.

TABLE B8. THE UNITED STATES' TRADE WITH
MAJOR POWERS

Pre–World War I

	Austria-Hungary	France	Germany	Italy	Japan	Russia	UK
1900	0.75	6.65	12.65	2.58	1.67	0.66	35.57
1905	1.86	6.99	12.45	2.91	3.55	1.14	26.17
1910	1.82	6.29	12.48	3.28	2.95	1.37	23.50
1913	0.97	7.29	13.80	3.62	4.69	1.46	21.38

Interwar Period

	France	Germany	Italy	Japan	Russia	UK
1920	5.99	3.53	2.81	6.33	0.13	21.26
1925	4.91	7.39	3.45	6.91	0.85	15.64
1931	4.99	5.69	2.89	8.20	2.87	13.31
1935	4.09	4.06	2.59	9.08	0.99	12.84
1938	4.08	4.47	2.20	7.80	2.00	13.18

Post–World War II

	China	France	Russia	UK
1950		2.67		4.91
1955		2.48	0.07	6.76
1960		3.20	0.18	7.31
1965		3.49		6.78
1970		3.38		6.00
1975	0.22	2.99		4.35
1980	1.05	3.41	0.42	5.09
1985	1.64	3.15	0.54	4.93
1990	2.51	3.58	0.50	5.05
1992	3.63	3.54	0.50	4.49

NOTES

CHAPTER 1

1. For purposes of simplification I use the term *liberal* here to refer to what Keohane (1993) terms *commercial liberals,* although liberals do not necessarily fit comfortably under a singular rubric. As Keohane states, "Commercial liberalism and republican liberalism—the belief that economic interdependence contributes to peace and that democracies are more peaceful, at least in some relationships, than nondemocracies—have long been important strains in liberal thinking" (271).

2. Hirschman ([1945] 1980, 10–11), provides a discussion of alternative views about whether trade itself constitutes mutual dependence.

3. "Sensitivity refers to the openness of a country to changes in other countries that are transmitted by a mutual interaction, vulnerability refers to the effects of changes in rules or policies" (quote from Gasiorowski 1986a, 24; see Keohane and Nye 1977, 12–13).

4. See Blumenfeld 1991 for an excellent assessment of the problems associated with the schools of thought and foreign policies promoting a strict dichotomy between notions of interdependence and dependence.

CHAPTER 2

1. It is important to note the distinctions in the way that classical and contemporary liberals portray the optimal role of the state. From a classical liberal perspective, permitting individuals and firms to pursue their interests is seen as the primary way in which the state can maximize national and global welfare. The literature tends to characterize classical liberalism as entailing a minimalist state in economic matters, but often overlooks the security functions ascribed to the state by classical liberals.

2. For a comprehensive history of this and related economic thought see Spiegel 1991; see de Wilde 1991 for a history of the interdependence tradition in political science.

3. An extensive review of trade theory is beyond the scope of this study. Interested readers should consult Bhagwati 1996, Kenen 1994, Takayama 1972, and Viner 1937 for an introduction to the literature.

4. See Sayrs 1990 for an extensive critique of Polachek's model.

5. See Baldwin 1985 for a discussion of various types of economic statecraft, including trade that may be used to substitute or supplement military options.

6. For a comprehensive review of dependency schools of thought see Blomström and Hettne 1984.

7. Advocates of South-South economic unions may view less significant, but

equal, economic linkages as a greater force for peace than are extensive relations under the guise of unequal exchange. According to this latter view, the linkages among developing states would eventually expand, providing increasing benefits (economic and political) in the long run and breaking the cycle of dependence on developed states.

CHAPTER 3

1. A comprehensive review of the theoretical and empirical findings concerning all the causes of interstate conflict and cooperation is beyond the scope of this study. Recent distillations of this literature include Bremer 1992b; Bremer and Cusack 1995; Geller and Singer 1998; Levy 1985, 1989; Midlarsky 1975; Vasquez 1993, 2000.

2. Most scholars agree that trade affects conflict and conflict affects trade, but vary over which relationship is dominant. Studies examining the mutual influence of trade and conflict include Polachek 1992 and Reuveny and Kang 1996. Barbieri and Levy (1999) examine the impact of war on trade and find variations across dyadic relationships. At the system level, Mansfield (1994) finds that war reduces trade.

3. Other scholars provide evidence of an inverse relationship between trade and political relations at the dyadic level, but view causation as flowing from politics to trade patterns (Dixon and Moon 1993; Gowa 1994; Pollins 1989a, 1989b).

4. Russett (1967) also provides evidence that increased trade leads to increased conflict during the post–World War II period. However, his study is primarily concerned with intraregional trade and conflict.

5. For example, empirical findings reveal that the impact of democracy varies at the monadic, dyadic, and system levels. The same may be true of trade, despite the cross-level predictions often associated with it.

6. In this study, interstate system membership is defined by the Correlates of War (COW) Project (Small and Singer 1982; Singer and Small 1994).

7. Details about my trade data project are discussed in appendix A.

8. When data were available from other sources, the IMF reports of zero trade were replaced with positive trade-values. I found no difference in the empirical results obtained by excluding, then including, the IMF's zero trade-values. In no cases did I substitute a value of zero for the missing trade-value codes.

9. Studies that assess the impact of trade on net conflict generally take the value of conflictual events minus cooperative events and are derived from Azar's *Conflict and Peace Data Bank* (COPDAB) (Azar 1979, 1985; Azar and Eckhart 1978; Azar and Havener 1976).

10. I refer to MIDs with the terms *dispute* and *disputes*.

11. The dependent variable, dispute, is really an event count, since it is conceivable that dyads may experience more than one dispute in a given year. Thus, a case could be made that an event-count model should be used in this analysis. I chose to dichotomize dispute, since the probability that a dyad would experience more than one MID in a given year is extremely small, and the occurrence of a second dispute

would probably be in violation of the assumption of independence between events. In addition, I argue that engaging in at least one dispute is sufficient to violate the trade-promotes-peace hypothesis.

12. Trade data for the pre–World War II period were derived from a database constructed by the author (see appendix A). For the post–World War II period, the International Monetary Fund's *Direction of Trade Statistics* (1991) was the primary data source. These data were made available by the Inter-university Consortium for Political and Social Research (ICPSR 7628) and were supplemented by a number of sources discussed at greater length in appendix A. The majority of data for GDP figures were obtained from World Bank 1995.

13. I calculate symmetry by one minus the absolute value of the difference of the two trade shares. The absolute value is used to reflect the irrelevance of the order in which the two trade shares are introduced into the equation, while subtracting this difference from one establishes the directional influence of the measure.

14. My desire to address the problem of multicollinearity was motivated, in a large part, by the comments of reviewers, who believed that using an interaction term that was highly collinear with the salience variable produced questionable empirical findings. However, I believe Friedrich (1982) offers a compelling case for including multiplicative terms that are highly collinear with one of their component elements. The findings presented here and those obtained when employing a non-standardized interaction term produce substantively similar findings.

15. Aitken (1973, 882) suggests that neighboring countries are expected to have an additional stimulus to trade because of the similarity of tastes and awareness of common interests. See Arad and Hirsch 1981 for a discussion of the ability of trade to promote peace among belligerent contiguous states.

16. Bremer (1992b) finds that geographically proximate states are the most likely to engage in militarized conflict. For summaries about the relationship between geography and conflict, see Goertz and Diehl 1992 and Gochman 1992. See Vasquez 1993 on the theoretical significance of this relationship.

17. I use the version of the contiguity data set that was revised by Philip Schafer in 1993.

18. In preliminary analyses I measure the influence of four separate categories of geographic proximity on conflict separately: (1) direct land contiguity (shared borders); (2) direct contiguity by sea (up to 150 miles of sea border); (3) indirect contiguity by land (shared border); and (4) indirect contiguity by sea (up to 150 miles). No significant difference in the trade-conflict relationship was identified across these separate categories.

19. See Ray 1995 and Chan 1997 for comprehensive reviews of the empirical literature on the democratic peace.

20. Rummel (1983, 1985) classifies states as libertarian only when economic freedoms exist, making it impossible to discern whether it is the political or economic ties that are responsible for his findings.

21. The addition of ten eliminates negative values from the index.

22. Gowa finds no significant relationship between alliance ties and trade pat-

terns in the pre–World War II period, but this may simply be explained by the small size of her sample. A stronger pattern relationship between alliances and trade might reveal itself in an investigation of a broader sample of relationships.

23. Bremer (1993, 237) finds that a dichotomous measure of alliance ties is sufficient to capture the effect of alliances on conflict, although slight variations exist in the effect of different alliance types.

24. Alan Sabrosky revised the version of the data set used.

25. All analyses were conducted using Stata 5.0 (Stata Corporation, 1996). For information about logit regression analysis and the interpretation of results, see Aldrich and Nelson 1984, King 1989, and Liao 1994.

CHAPTER 4

1. For discussions of ordered logit analysis, see King 1989; Liao 1994; Maddala 1983; Greene 1993; Zavoina and McElvey 1975.

CHAPTER 5

1. Data for the period 1869 through 1970 were taken from U.S. Bureau of the Census 1975, Series E 135, 210–11. These data were supplemented for the years 1960 through 1994 with data from the *World Almanac* and *Book of Facts* (1995, 492). See Barbieri and Bremer 1998 for a more complete discussion of this adjustment procedure.

2. Papayoanou (1997, 1999) also considers nontrade ties in evaluating economic interdependence between the major powers prior to World War I.

3. As discussed in appendix A, I rely on reports from each partner in deriving the dyadic measures. Therefore, the figures reported below might vary from published reports that rely on the statistics reported by one country. As I also discuss in appendix A, the data reported below are derived from several publications, and inconsistencies in reports of trading partners and across publications are common.

4. See Barbieri and Levy 1999 for a discussion of trade between enemies during and after the war. There, I argue that trade ties between wartime adversaries might expand once the war has ended. Some notable examples are seen in the United States' relationships with Japan and Germany. Again, we must consider the fact that trade dependence might still decline relative to earlier periods, since all states in the post–World War II period are better able to divert trade patterns more easily than they were in earlier periods of history.

APPENDIX A

1. Yates (1959, chap. 2) provides a comprehensive discussion of problems posed by trade data limitations.

2. Comparisons were made to empirical results obtained by excluding and including major war years, and no significant differences were observed.

3. Information about the *Polity II* exchange rates was acquired through a telephone conversation with Gurr (approximately April 1994). He informed me that the majority of exchange rates found in the database were originally collected by the COW Project. However, some revisions were made to the COW figures, but these cases are not documented in the Codebook. Philip Schafer (telephone conversation, April 1994), who works on the COW Project, informed me that the COW exchange rates were collected from *The Statesman's Yearbook*. When currency names were missing, I could assume that they corresponded to the names listed as the national currency with the yearbook. Unfortunately, I uncovered many instances where the exchange rates reported in *Polity II* did not correspond to the rates appearing in *The Statesman's Yearbook*. It is unclear whether these discrepancies correspond to the adjustments made by Gurr or whether they include an error in reporting. Since the answer was unclear, I choose to rely on alternative sources for exchange rates when currency names were absent from *Polity II*.

4. Some of these sources were also used for the pre–World War II period.

BIBLIOGRAPHY

Aitken, Norman D. 1973. "The Effect of the EEC and EFTA on European Trade: A Temporal Cross-Section Analysis." *American Economic Review* 63, no. 5: 881–92.

Aldrich, John Herbert, and Forrest D. Nelson. 1984. *Linear Probability, Logit, and Probit Models.* Sage University Papers Series. Quantitative Applications in the Social Sciences; 07–045. Beverly Hills, CA: Sage.

Amin, Samir. 1977. *Imperialism and Unequal Development.* New York: Monthly Review Press.

Anderton, Charles H., and John R. Carter. 2001. "The Impact of War on Trade: An Interrupted Times-Series Study." *Journal of Peace Research* 38, no. 4: 445–57.

Angell, Norman. [1911] 1972. *The Great Illusion: A Study of the Relation of Military Power to National Advantage.* New York and London: Garland.

Arad, Ruth W., and Seev Hirsch. 1981. "Peacemaking and Vested Interests: International Economic Transactions." *International Studies Quarterly* 25:439–68.

Axelrod, Robert M. 1984. *The Evolution of Cooperation.* New York: Basic Books.

Azar, Edward E. 1979. "Peace Amidst Development: A Conceptual Agenda for Conflict and Peace Research." *International Interactions* 62, no. 2: 123–43.

———. 1985. "Protracted International Conflicts: Ten Propositions." *International Interactions* 12, no. 1: 59–70.

Azar, Edward E., and William Eckhart. 1978. "Major World Cooperation Events, 1945–1975." *International Interactions* 5, no. 2: 203–39.

Azar, Edward E., and Thomas Havener. 1976. "Discontinuities in the Symbolic Environment: A Problem in Scaling." *International Interactions* 2, no. 2: 231–46.

Baldwin, David A. 1985. *Economic Statecraft.* Princeton: Princeton University Press.

———, ed. 1993. *Neorealism and Neoliberalism: The Contemporary Debate, New Directions in World Politics.* New York: Columbia University Press.

Balogh, Thomas. 1963. *Unequal Partners.* Vol. 1: *The Theoretical Framework.* Oxford: Basil Blackwell.

Banks, Arthur S. 1979. "Cross-National Time-Series Data Archive." Center for Social Analysis, State University of New York at Binghamton.

Baran, Paul A. 1957. *The Political Economy of Growth.* New York: Monthly Review Press.

Barbieri, Katherine. 1995. "Economic Interdependence and Militarized Interstate Conflict, 1870–1985." Ph.D. diss., Department of Political Science, State University of New York at Binghamton.

———. 1996a. "Economic Interdependence: A Path to Peace or a Source of Interstate Conflict?" *Journal of Peace Research* 33:29–49.

———. 1996b. "Interdependence and the Characteristics of Conflict." Paper presented at the Annual Meeting of the American Political Science Association, San Francisco, August 28–September 1.

————. 1996c. "Explaining Discrepant Findings in the Trade-Conflict Literature." Presented at the Annual Meeting of the International Studies Association, San Diego, April 16–21.

————. 1997. "Risky Business: The Impact of Trade Linkages on Interstate Conflict, 1870–1985." In *Enforcing Cooperation: 'Risky' States and Intergovernmental Management of Conflict*, ed. Gerald Schneider and Patricia A. Weitsman, 202–31. London: Macmillan.

————. 1998. "International Trade and Conflict: The Debatable Relationship." Presented at the Annual Meeting of the International Studies Association, Minneapolis, March 18–21.

Barbieri, Katherine, and Stuart A. Bremer. 1995. "Economic Interdependence and Dispute Duration, 1870–1985." Paper presented at the Annual Meeting of the Peace Science Society, Columbus, OH, October 13–15.

————. 1998. "Economic Interdependence and Dispute Duration, 1870–1992." Manuscript.

Barbieri, Katherine, and Jack S. Levy. 1999. "Sleeping with the Enemy: The Impact of War on Trade." *Journal of Peace Research* 36, no. 4: 463–80.

Barbieri, Katherine, and Gerald Schneider. 1999. "Globalization and Peace: Assessing New Directions in the Study of Trade and Conflict." *Journal of Peace Research* 36, no. 4: 387–404.

Beck, Nathaniel, Jonathan N. Katz, and Richard Tucker. 1998. "Taking Time Seriously: Time-Series-Cross-Section Analysis with a Binary Dependent Variable." *American Journal of Political Science* 42, no. 4: 1260–88.

Bercheid, Ellen, Mark Snyder, and Allen Omoto. 1989. "Issues in Studying Close Relationships: Conceptualizing and Measuring Closeness." In *Close Relationships*, ed. Clyde Hendrick, 39–62. Newbury Park, CA: Sage.

Bhagwati, Jagdish N., ed. 1996. *International Trade: Selected Readings.* 2d ed. Cambridge: MIT Press.

Bidwell, Robin Leonard. 1970. *Currency Conversion Tables: A Hundred Years of Change.* London: Rex Collings.

Blainey, Geoffrey. 1973. *The Causes of War.* New York: Free Press.

Blanchard, Jean-Marc F., and Norrin M. Ripsman. 1994. "Peace through Economic Interdependence? Appeasement in 1936." Paper presented at the Annual Meeting of the American Political Science Association, New York, Sept. 1–14.

Blomström, Magnus, and Björn Hettne. 1984. *Development Theory in Transition: The Dependency Debate and Beyond. Third World Responses.* London: Zed Books.

Blumenfeld, Jesmond, and Institute of International Affairs. 1991. *Economic Interdependence in Southern Africa: From Conflict to Cooperation.* New York: St. Martin's.

Boulding, Kenneth Ewart. 1962. *Conflict and Defense: A General Theory.* New York: Harper.

Brawley, Mark. 1993. "Regime Types, Markers, and War. The Importance of Pervasive Rents in Foreign Policy." *Comparative Political Studies* 26, no. 2: 178–97.

Bremer, Stuart A. 1980. "National Capabilities and War Proneness." In *The Corre-

lates of War II: Testing Some Realpolitik Models, ed. J. David Singer, 57–83. New
York: Free Press.

———. 1992a. "Are Democracies Less Likely to Join Wars?" Paper presented at the
Annual Meeting of the American Political Science Association, Chicago, September 3–6.

———. 1992b. "Dangerous Dyads: Conditions Affecting the Likelihood of Interstate War, 1816–1965." *Journal of Conflict Resolution* 36, no. 2: 309–41.

———. 1993. "Democracy and Militarized Interstate Conflict, 1816–1965." *International Interactions* 18:231–50.

Bremer, Stuart A., and Thomas R. Cusack, eds. 1995. *The Process of War: Advancing the Scientific Study of War.* Luxembourg: Gordon and Breach.

Brown, Keith C., ed. 1965. *Hobbes Studies.* Cambridge: Harvard University Press.

Bueno de Mesquita, Bruce. 1981. *The War Trap.* New Haven: Yale University Press.

Buzan, Barry. 1984. "Economic Structure and International Security: The Limits of the Liberal Case." *International Organization* 38, no. 4: 597–624.

Cardoso, Fernando Henrique, and Enzo Faletto. 1979. *Dependency and Development in Latin America.* Berkeley: University of California Press.

Chan, Steven. 1997. "In Search of Democratic Peace: Problems and Promise." *Mershon International Studies Review* 41, no. 1: 59–92.

Chatterji, Manas, and Linda Rennie Forcey. 1992. *Disarmament, Economic Conversion, and Management of Peace.* New York: Praeger.

Choucri, Nazli, and Robert Carver North. 1975. *Nations in Conflict: National Growth and International Violence.* San Francisco: W. H. Freeman.

———. 1989. "Lateral Pressure in International Relations: Concept and Theory." In *Handbook of War Studies,* ed. Manus I. Midlarsky, 289–326. Boston: Unwin Hyman.

Cohen, Benjamin J. 1973. *The Question of Imperialism: The Political Economy of Dominance and Dependence.* Political Economy of International Relations Series. New York: Basic Books.

Cooper, Richard N. 1968. *The Economics of Interdependence: Economic Policy in the Atlantic Community.* New York: McGraw-Hill, for the Council on Foreign Relations.

Coser, Lewis A. 1956. *The Functions of Social Conflict.* Glencoe, IL: Free Press.

de Rohan, Henri. 1995. *De l'intérêt des princes et des états de la chrétienté.* Ed. Christian Lazzeri. Paris: Presses Universitaires de France.

de Vries, Michael. 1990. "Interdependence, Cooperation, and Conflict: An Empirical Analysis." *Journal of Peace Research* 27, no. 4:429–44.

de Wilde, Jaap. 1991. *Saved from Oblivion: Interdependence Theory in the First Half of the Twentieth Century. A Study of the Causality between War and Complex Interdependence.* Aldershot: Dartmouth.

Deane, Herbert A. 1963. *The Political and Social Ideas of St. Augustine.* New York: Columbia University Press.

Deutsch, Karl Wolfgang, Sidney Burrel, Robert Kann, Maurice Lee, Martin Lichterman, Raymond Lindgren, Francis Loewenheim, and Richard van Wagener. 1957.

Political Community and the North Atlantic Area: International Organization in the Light of Historical Experience. Princeton: Princeton University Press.

Dixon, William. 1993. "Democracy and the Management of International Conflict." *Journal of Conflict Resolution* 37, no. 1: 42–68.

———. 1994. "Democracy and the Peaceful Settlement of International Conflict." *American Political Science Review* 88:14–32.

Dixon, William, and Bruce Moon. 1993. "Political Similarity and American Foreign Trade Patterns." *Political Research Quarterly* 46:5–25.

Domke, William Kinkade. 1988. *War and the Changing Global System.* New Haven: Yale University Press.

Dorussen, Han. 1999. "Balance of Power Revisited: A Multi-Country Model of Trade and Conflict." *Journal of Peace Research* 36, no. 4: 443 62.

Dos Santos, Theodonio. 1970. "The Structure of Dependence." *American Economic Review* 60, no. 2: 231–36.

Doyle, Michael W. 1997. *Ways of War and Peace: Realism, Liberalism, and Socialism.* New York: Norton.

Emmanuel, Arghiri. 1972. *Unequal Exchange: A Study of the Imperialism of Trade, Modern Reader,* Pb-188. New York: Monthly Review Press.

Enterline, Andrew. 1995. "Regime Transitions and Militarized Interstate Disputes, 1816–1986." Manuscript, Binghamton.

Europa Publications. 1960–96. *The Europa Year Book.* Vol. I. *Europe.* Annual. London: Europa.

Evans, Peter B. 1979. *Dependent Development: The Alliance of Multinational, State, and Local Capital in Brazil.* Princeton: Princeton University Press.

Forbes, Hugh D. 1997. *Ethnic Conflict: Commerce, Culture, and the Contact Hypothesis.* New Haven: Yale University Press.

Frank, Andre Gunder. 1967. *Capitalism and Underdevelopment in Latin America: Historical Studies of Chile and Brazil.* New York: Monthly Review Press.

Freud, Sigmund. 1938. *A General Introduction to Psycho-Analysis.* New York: Garden City. Cited in Lewis Coser, *The Functions of Social Conflict,* 61–62. New York: Free Press, 1948.

Freud, Sigmund. 1948. *Group Psychology and the Analysis of the Ego.* London: Hogarth Press, 54–55. Cited in Lewis Coser, *The Functions of Social Conflict,* 61–62. New York: Free Press, 1948.

Friedrich, Robert J. 1982. "In Defense of Multiplicative Terms in Multiple Regression Equations." *American Journal of Political Science* 26, no. 4: 797–833.

Furtado, Celso. 1963. *The Economic Growth of Brazil: A Survey from Colonial to Modern Times.* Berkeley: University of California Press.

Galtung, Johan. 1971. "A Structural Theory of Imperialism." *Journal of Peace Research* 8, no. 2: 81–117.

Gasiorowski, Mark. 1986a. "Economic Interdependence and International Conflict: Some Cross-National Evidence." *International Studies Quarterly* 30:23–38.

———. 1986b. "Structure and Dynamics in International Interdependence." In *Dependency Theory and the Return to High Politics,* ed. Mary Ann Tétreault and Charles F. Abel, 71–100. New York: Greenwood.

Gasiorowski, Mark J., and Solomon W. Polachek. 1982. "Conflict and Interdependence: East-West Trade and Linkages in the Era of Detente." *Journal of Conflict Resolution* 26:709–29.

Geller, Daniel S. 1993. "Power Differentials and War in Rival Dyads." *International Studies Quarterly* 37, no. 2: 173–94.

Geller, Daniel S., and J. David Singer. 1998. *Nations at War: A Scientific Study of International Conflict.* Cambridge Studies in International Relations, 58. Cambridge: Cambridge University Press.

Gilbert, Felix. 1965. *Machiavelli and Guicciardini: Politics and History in Sixteenth-Century Florence.* Princeton: Princeton University Press.

Gleditsch, Nils Petter, and Håvard Hegre. 1997. "Peace and Democracy: Three Levels of Analysis." *Journal of Conflict Resolution* 41:283–310.

Gochman, Charles. 1992. "Interstate Metrics since the Congress of Vienna." In *The New Geopolitics,* ed. Michael D. Ward. Philadelphia: Gordon and Breach.

Gochman, Charles S., and Zeev Maoz. 1984. "Militarized Interstate Disputes, 1816–1976." *Journal of Conflict Resolution* 28, no. 4: 585–615.

Gochman, Charles S., and Alan Ned Sabrosky, eds. 1990. *Prisoners of War? Nation-States in the Modern Era.* Lexington, MA: Lexington Books.

Goertz, Gary, and Paul F. Diehl. 1992. *Territorial Changes and International Conflict.* London: Routledge.

Gowa, Joanne S. 1994. *Allies, Adversaries, and International Trade.* Princeton: Princeton University Press.

Greene, William H. 1993. *Econometric Analysis.* 2d ed. Englewood Cliffs, NJ: Prentice-Hall.

Grieco, Joseph M. 1990. *Cooperation among Nations: Europe, America, and Non-Tariff Barriers to Trade.* Cornell Studies in Political Economy. Ithaca: Cornell University Press.

Grieco, Joseph M., Robert Powell, and Duncan Snidal. 1993. "The Relative-Gains Problem for International Cooperation. Comment on Snidal and Powell. With Responses." *American Political Science Review* 87, no. 3: 729–43.

Gurr, Ted Robert. 1970. *Why Men Rebel.* Princeton: Princeton University Press.

Gurr, Ted Robert, Keith Jaggers, and Will H. Moore. 1989. *Polity II Codebook.* Boulder: University of Colorado.

Haas, Ernst B. 1958. *The Uniting of Europe: Political, Social, and Economic Forces, 1950–1957.* Stanford, CA: Stanford University Press.

———. 1964. *Beyond the Nation-State: Functionalism and International Organization.* Stanford, CA: Stanford University Press.

Heilbroner, Robert L. 1973. "The Paradox of Progress: Decline and Decay in the Wealth of Nations." *Journal of the History of Ideas* 34, no. 2: 243–62.

Hendrick, Clyde, ed. 1989. *Close Relationships.* Newbury Park, CA: Sage.

Higham, Charles. 1983. *Trading with the Enemy: An Exposé of the Nazi-American Money Plot, 1933–1949.* New York: Delacorte.

Hirsch, Leonard Paul. 1986. "Incorporation into the World Economy: Empirical Tests of Dependency Theory." In *Dependency Theory and the Return of High Politics,* ed. Mary Ann Tétreault and Charles Abel, 101–24. New York: Greenwood.

Hirschman, Albert O. [1945] 1980. *National Power and the Structure of Foreign Trade.* Publications of the Bureau of Business and Economic Research, University of California. Berkeley and Los Angeles: University of California Press.

———. 1977. *The Passions and the Interests: Political Arguments for Capitalism before Its Triumph.* Princeton: Princeton University Press.

———. 1982. "Rival Interpretations of Market Society: Civilizing, Destructive, or Feeble?" *Journal of Economic Literature* 20:1463–1514.

Hobson, John A. [1902] 1954. *Imperialism: A Study.* London: G. Allen and Unwin.

Houweling, Henk, and Jan Siccama. 1991. "Power Transitions and Critical Points as Predictors of Great Power War: Toward a Synthesis." *Journal of Conflict Resolution* 35:642–58.

Hower, Gretchen. 1990. "The Dynamics of Hostile and Cooperative Behavior." Ph.D. diss., University of Illinois.

Hughes, Barry B. 1972. "Transaction Analysis: The Impact of Operationalization." *International Organization* 25:132–45.

———. 1997. *Continuity and Change in World Politics: Competing Perspectives.* 3d ed. Upper Saddle River, NJ: Prentice-Hall.

Inter-University Consortium for Political and Social Research. 1991. "Direction of Trade Codebook (ICPSR 7628)." Ann Arbor: Inter-University Consortium for Political and Social Research.

International Monetary Fund. 1956–98. *International Financial Statistics.* Monthly. Washington, DC: IMF Statistics Department.

———. 1991. *Direction of Trade Statistics 1991 Yearbook.* Washington, DC: International Monetary Fund.

Irwin, Douglas. 1996. *Against the Tide: An Intellectual History of Free Trade.* Princeton: Princeton University Press.

Ivens, Michael, and Reginald Dunstan, eds. 1967. *The Case for Capitalism.* London: Michael Joseph.

Jaggers, Keith, and Ted Robert Gurr. 1995. "Tracking Democracy's Third Wave with the Polity III Data." *Journal of Peace Research* 32, no. 4: 469–82.

———. 1996. *POLITY III: Regime Change and Political Authority, 1800–1994.* [computer file] (Study #6695). 2d ICPSR version. Boulder, CO: Keith Jaggers/College Park, MD: Ted Robert Gurr [producers], 1995. Ann Arbor, MI: Inter-University Consortium for Political and Social Research [distributor], 1996.

Jalée, Pierre. 1977. *How Capitalism Works: Modern Reader.* New York: Monthly Review Press.

Jones, Daniel M., Stuart A. Bremer, and J. David Singer. 1996. "Militarized Interstate Disputes, 1816–1992: Rationale, Coding Rules, and Empirical Applications." *Conflict Management and Peace Science* 15, no. 2: 163–213.

Keegan, John. 1993. *A History of Warfare.* London: Hutchinson.

Kegley, Charles W., and Neil R. Richardson. 1980. "Trade Dependence and Foreign Policy Compliance: A Longitudinal Analysis." *International Studies Quarterly* 24, no. 2: 191–222.

Kegley, Charles W., and Eugene R. Wittkopf. 1995. *World Politics: Trend and Transformation.* 5th ed. New York: St. Martin's.

Kenen, Peter B. 1994. *The International Economy*. 3d ed. Cambridge: Cambridge University Press.

Kennedy, Peter. 1998. *A Guide to Econometrics*. 4th ed. Cambridge: MIT Press.

Keohane, Robert O. 1993. "Institutional Theory and the Realist Challenge after the Cold War." In *Neorealism and Neoliberalism: The Contemporary Debate*, ed. David A. Baldwin, 269–301. New York: Columbia University Press.

Keohane, Robert O., and Joseph S. Nye. 1977. *Power and Interdependence: World Politics in Transition*. Boston: Little, Brown.

King, Gary. 1989. *Unifying Political Methodology: The Likelihood Theory of Statistical Inference*. Cambridge: Cambridge University Press.

Kirshner, Julius, ed. 1974. *Business, Banking, and Economic Thought in Late Medieval and Early Modern Europe: Selected Studies of Raymond De Roover*. Chicago: University of Chicago Press.

Koekkoek, Ad, L. B. M. Mennes, and Jagdish N. Bhagwati. 1991. *International Trade and Global Development: Essays in Honour of Jagdish Bhagwati*. London and New York: Routledge.

Kydd, Rachael M. 1964. *Reason and Conduct in Hume's Treatise*. New York: Russell and Russell.

League of Nations. 1910–40. "Memorandum on International Trade and Balance of Payments Statistics." Geneva: League of Nations.

Lenin, Vladimir Ilich. [1919] 1990. *Imperialism, the Highest Stage of Capitalism*. Reprint. New York: International.

Lessnoff, Michael H. 1994. *The Spirit of Capitalism and the Protestant Ethic: An Enquiry into the Weber Thesis*. London: Edward Elgar.

Levy, Jack S. 1985. "Theories of General War." *World Politics* 37, no. 3: 344–74.

———. 1989. "The Causes of War: A Review of Theories and Evidence." In *Behavior, Society, and Nuclear War*, vol. 1, ed. Phillip E. Tetlock, Jo L. Husbands, Robert Jervis, Paul C. Stern, and Charles Tilly, 212–333. New York and Oxford: Oxford University Press.

Liao, Tim Futing. 1994. *Interpreting Probability Models: Logit, Probit, and Other Generalized Linear Models*. Sage University Papers Series. Quantitative Applications in the Social Sciences; No. 07–101. Thousand Oaks, CA: Sage.

Liberman, Peter. 1996. *Does Conquest Pay? The Exploitation of Occupied Industrial Societies*. Princeton: Princeton University Press.

Maddala, G. S. 1983. *Limited-Dependent and Qualitative Variables in Econometrics*. Econometric Society Monographs in Quantitative Economics, no. 3. Cambridge: Cambridge University Press.

Maddison, Angus. 1995. *Monitoring the World Economy, 1820–1992*. Development Centre Studies. Paris: Development Centre of the Organisation for Economic Co-operation and Development.

Maher, Paul. 1972. *Soviet and East European Foreign Trade, 1946–1969*. Bloomington: Indiana University Press.

Mansfield, Edward D. 1994. *Power, Trade, and War*. Princeton: Princeton University Press.

Mansfield, Edward D., and Jack Snyder. 1995. "Democratization and War." *Foreign Affairs* 74, no. 3: 79–97.

Maoz, Zeev. 1996. *Domestic Sources of Global Change.* Ann Arbor: University of Michigan Press.

Maoz, Zeev, and Nasrin Abdolali. 1989. "Regime Types and International Conflict." *Journal of Conflict Resolution* 33:3–35.

Maoz, Zeev, and Bruce M. Russett. 1993. "Normative and Structural Causes of the Democratic Peace, 1945–1986." *American Political Science Review* 87, no. 3: 624–38.

Marrese, Michael, and Jan Va'ous. 1983. "Unconventional Gains from Trade." *Journal of Comparative Economics* 7, no. 4: 382–99.

Marx, Karl. 1848. "On the Question of Free Trade." Speech to the Democratic Association of Brussels at its public meeting of January 9. Marx and Engels Internet Archive, <www.marxists.org> (accessed May 2001).

———. 1887. *Capital, a Critique of Political Economy,* vol. 1, ed. Friedrich Engels. Trans. Samuel Moore and Edward Bibbins Aveling. Moscow: Progress Publishers. Reprint, New York: Modern Library, 1906.

Mastanduno, Michael. 1993. "Do Relative Gains Matter?" In *Neorealism and Neoliberalism: The Contemporary Debate,* ed. David A. Baldwin, 250–69. New York: Columbia University Press.

Meek, Ronald L. 1958. "The Economics of Control Prefigured by Sir James Steuart." *Science and Society* 22:289–305.

Midlarsky, Manus I. 1975. *On War: Political Violence in the International System.* New York: Free Press.

———. 1989. *Handbook of War Studies.* Boston: Unwin Hyman.

Mill, John Stuart. 1848a. *Principles of Political Economy, with Some of Their Applications to Social Philosophy.* London: J. W. Parker.

———. 1848b. *A System of Logic, Ratiocinative and Inductive; Being a Connected View of the Principles of Evidence and the Methods of Scientific Investigation.* New York: Harper and Brothers.

Mitchell, Brian R. 1982. *International Historical Statistics: Africa and Asia.* New York: New York University Press.

———. 1983. *International Historical Statistics: The Americas and Australasia.* Detroit: Gale Research.

Mitrany, David. 1964. *A Working Peace System.* Chicago: Quadrangle.

Montesquieu, Charles de Secondat, baron de. [1749] 1989. *The Spirit of the Laws.* Trans. Anne M. Cohler, Basia C. Miller, and Harold Stone. Cambridge and New York: Cambridge University Press.

Morgan, T. Clifton, and Sally Howard Campbell. 1991. "Domestic Structure, Decisional Constraints and War: So Why Kant Democracies Fight?" *Journal of Conflict Resolution* 35:187–211.

Morgan, T. Clifton, and Valerie L. Schwebach. 1992. "Take Two Democracies and Call Me in the Morning: A Prescription for Peace?" *International Interactions* 17, no. 4: 305–20.

Morgenthau, Hans Joachim. 1948. *Politics among Nations: The Struggle for Power and Peace.* New York: Knopf.

Morrow, James D. 1999. "How Could Trade Affect Conflict?" *Journal of Peace Research* 36, no. 4: 481–89.

Myrdal, Gunnar. 1957. *Economic Theory and Under-Developed Regions.* London: G. Duckworth.

Neff, Stephen. 1990. *Friends but No Allies: Economic Liberalism and the Law of Nations.* New York: Columbia University Press.

Nye, Joseph S. 1968. "Comparative Regional Integration: Concept and Measurement." *International Organization* 22:855–80.

Oneal, John R., Frances H. Oneal, Zeev Maoz, and Bruce M. Russett. 1996. "The Liberal Peace: Interdependence, Democracy, and International Conflict, 1950–85." *Journal of Peace Research* 33, no. 1: 11–28.

Oneal, John R., and James Lee Ray. 1997. "New Tests of the Democratic Peace: Controlling for Economic Interdependence, 1950–85." *Political Research Quarterly* 50, no. 4: 751–75.

Oneal, John R., and Bruce M. Russett. 1997. "The Classical Liberals Were Right: Democracy, Interdependence, and Conflict, 1950–1985." *International Studies Quarterly* 41, no. 2: 267–95.

———. 1999. "Assessing the Liberal Peace with Alternative Specifications: Trade Still Reduces Conflict." *Journal of Peace Research* 36, no. 4: 423–42.

Onimode, Bade. 1985. *An Introduction to Marxist Political Economy.* London: Zed Books.

Organski, A. F. K., and Jacek Kugler. 1980. *The War Ledger.* Chicago: University of Chicago Press.

Papayoanou, Paul A. 1997. "Economic Interdependence and the Balance of Power." *International Studies Quarterly* 41, no. 1: 113–40.

———. 1999. *Power Ties: Economic Interdependence, Balancing, and War.* Ann Arbor: University of Michigan Press.

Pascal, Blaise. 1941. *Pensées: The Provincial Letters.* New York: Modern Library.

Pearce, David W., ed. 1992. *The MIT Dictionary of Modern Economics.* 4th ed. Cambridge: MIT Press.

Peres, Shimon, and Arye Naor. 1993. *The New Middle East.* New York: Henry Holt.

Polachek, Solomon W. 1980. "Conflict and Trade." *Journal of Conflict Resolution* 24:55–78.

———. 1992. "Conflict and Trade: An Economics Approach to Political International Interactions." In *Economics of Arms Reduction and the Peace Process,* ed. Walter Isard and Charles H. Anderton, 89–120. Amsterdam: North Holland.

———. 1997. "Why Democracies Cooperate More and Fight Less." *Review of International Economics* 5, no. 3: 295–309.

Polachek, Solomon, Yuan-Ching Chang, and John Robst. 1997."Liberalism and Interdependence." Department of Economics, State University of New York at Binghamton.

Polachek, Solomon, and Judy McDonald. 1992. "Strategic Trade and the Incentive for Cooperation." In *Disarmament, Economic Conversion, and Peace Management,* ed. Manas Chatterji and Linda Rennie Forcey. New York: Praeger.

Polachek, Solomon W., John Robst, and Yuan-Ching Chang. 1999. "Liberalism and Interdependence: Extending the Trade-Conflict Model." *Journal of Peace Research* 36, no. 4: 405–22.

Pollins, Brian M. 1989a. "Does Trade Still Follow the Flag?" *American Political Science Review* 83, no. 2: 465–80.

———. 1989b. "Conflict, Cooperation, and Commerce: The Effect of International Political Interactions on Bilateral Trade Flows." *American Journal of Political Science* 33, no. 3: 737–61.

Powell, Robert. 1991. "Absolute and Relative Gains in International Relations Theory." *American Political Science Review* 85, no. 4: 1303–20.

Prebisch, Raul. 1950. *The Economic Development of Latin America and Its Principal Problems.* New York: United Nations.

Pruitt, Dean G., and Jeffrey Z. Rubin. 1986. *Social Conflict: Escalation, Stalemate, and Settlement.* New York: Random House.

Putnam, Robert. 1988. "Diplomacy and Domestic Politics: The Logic of Two-Level Games." *International Interactions* 42:427–60.

Ray, James Lee. 1995. *Democracy and International Conflict: An Evaluation of the Democratic Peace Proposition.* Studies in International Relations. Columbia: University of South Carolina Press.

Ray, James Lee, and Yijia Wang. 1998. "Integrating Levels of Analysis in World Politics: Increased Utility or Exercises in Futility?" Paper presented at the Annual Meeting of the American Political Science Association, Boston, September 3–6.

Raymond, Gregory A. 1994. "Democracies, Disputes, and Third-Party Intermediaries." *Journal of Conflict Resolution* 38:24–42.

———. 1995. "Treaties, Trust, and Conflict Escalation." Paper presented at the Annual Meeting of the International Studies Association, Chicago.

Reuveny, Rafael, and Heejon Kang. 1996. "International Trade, Political Conflict/Cooperation, and Granger Causality." *American Journal of Political Science* 40, no. 3: 943–70.

Richardson, Lewis Frye. 1960. *Statistics of Deadly Quarrels.* Pacific Grove, CA: Boxwood.

Ripsman, Norrin M., and Jean-Marc F. Blanchard. 1996/97. "Commercial Liberalism under Fire: Evidence from 1914 and 1936." *Security Studies* 6, no. 2: 4–50.

Rogowski, Ronald. 1989. *Commerce and Coalitions: How Trade Affects Domestic Political Alignments.* Princeton: Princeton University Press.

Rosecrance, Richard N. 1986. *The Rise of the Trading State: Commerce and Conquest in the Modern World.* New York: Basic Books.

Rosecrance, Richard N., and Arthur A. Stein, eds. 1993. *The Domestic Bases of Grand Strategy.* Cornell Studies in Security Affairs. Ithaca: Cornell University Press.

Rosenberg, Nathan. 1965. "Adam Smith on the Division of Labour: Two Views or One?" *Economica* 32:127–39.

———. 1968. "Adam Smith, Consumer Tastes, and Economic Growth." *Journal of Political Economy* 76:361–74.

Rubin, Jeffrey Z., Dean G. Pruitt, and Sung Hee Kim. 1994. *Social Conflict: Escalation, Stalemate, and Settlement.* New York: McGraw-Hill.

Rudé, George. 1962. *Wilkes and Liberty: A Social Study of 1763–1774.* Oxford: Clarendon.

Rummel, Rudolph J. 1983. "Libertarianism and International Violence." *Journal of Conflict Resolution* 27:27–71.

———. 1985. "Libertarian Propositions on Violence within and between Nations." *Journal of Conflict Resolution* 29:419–55.

Russett, Bruce M. 1967. *International Regions and the International System: A Study in Political Ecology.* Rand McNally Series in Comparative Government and International Politics. Chicago: Rand McNally.

———. 1983. "Prosperity and Peace: Presidential Address." *International Studies Quarterly* 27:381–87.

———. 1993. *Grasping the Democratic Peace: Principles for a Post–Cold War World.* Princeton: Princeton University Press.

Savage, I. Richard, and Karl W. Deutsch. 1960. "A Statistical Model of the Gross Analysis of Transaction Flows." *Econometrica* 28, no. 3: 551–72.

Sayrs, Lois W. 1990. "Expected Utility and Peace Science: An Assessment of Trade and Conflict." *Conflict Management and Peace Science* 12:17–44.

Schumpeter, Joseph A. 1954. *History of Economic Ideas.* New York: Oxford University.

Seers, Dudley. 1963. "The Limitations of the Special Case." *Bulletin of the Oxford Institute of Economics and Statistics* 25, no. 2.

Selfridge, H. Gordon. 1918. *The Romance of Commerce.* London: Bodley Heard.

Senese, Paul D. 1997. "Between Dispute and War: The Effect of Joint Democracy on Interstate Conflict Escalation." *Journal of Politics* 59, no. 1: 1–27.

Simmel, Georg. 1955. *Conflict.* Glencoe, IL: Free Press.

Singer, Hans W. 1950. "The Distribution of Gains between Investing and Borrowing Countries." *American Economic Review* 40, no. 2: 473–85.

Singer, J. David. 1961. "The Level-of-Analysis Problem in International Relations." *World Politics* 14, no. 1 (Oct.): 77–92.

Singer, J. David, and Paul F. Diehl, eds. 1990. *Measuring the Correlates of War.* Ann Arbor: University of Michigan Press.

Singer, J. David, and Melvin Small. 1994. "Correlates of War Project: International and Civil War Data, 1816–1992 (ICPSR 9905)." Ann Arbor, MI: Inter-University Consortium for Political and Social Research.

Small, Melvin, and J. David Singer. 1969. "Formal Alliances, 1816–1965: An Extension of the Basic Data." *Journal of Peace Research* 6, no. 3: 257–82.

———. 1982. *Resort to Arms: International and Civil Wars, 1816–1980.* 2d ed. Beverly Hills, CA: Sage.

Smith, Adam. [1776] 1937. *An Inquiry into the Nature and Causes of the Wealth of Nations.* New York: Random House.

Snidal, Duncan. 1991. "International Cooperation among Relative Gains Maximizers." *International Studies Quarterly* 35, no. 4: 387–402.

———. 1993. "Relative Gains and the Pattern of International Cooperation." In *Neorealism and Neoliberalism: The Contemporary Debate,* ed. David A. Baldwin, 170–208. New York: Columbia University Press.

Soroos, Marvin. 1977. "Behavior between Nations." *Peace Research Reviews* 7, no. 2: 1–107.

Spiegel, Henry William. 1991. *The Growth of Economic Thought.* 3d ed. Durham: Duke University Press.

Stata Statistical Software Version 5.0. Stata Corporation, College Station, TX.

State Statistical Bureau of the People's Republic of China, Renze Zhang, ed. 1990. *China Statistical Yearbook.* New York: Praeger.

The Statesman's Yearbook. 1864–1940. London: Macmillan.

Stein, Arthur A. 1990. *Why Nations Cooperate: Circumstance and Choice in International Relations.* Ithaca: Cornell University Press.

Steuart, Sir James. 1966. *An Inquiry into the Principles of Political Economy.* Vol. 1. Chicago: University of Chicago Press.

Stiglitz, Joseph E. 1986. *Economics of the Public Sector.* New York: W. W. Norton.

Strauss, Leo. 1963. *The Political Philosophy of Hobbes: Its Basis and Its Genesis.* Trans. Elsa M. Sinclair. Chicago: University of Chicago Press.

Sweezy, Paul Marlor. 1942. *The Theory of Capitalist Development: Principles of Marxian Political Economy.* New York: Monthly Review.

Takayama, Akira. 1972. *International Trade: An Approach to the Theory.* New York: Holt, Rinehart and Winston.

Tétreault, Mary Ann, and Charles Abel, eds. 1986. *Dependency Theory and the Return of High Politics.* New York: Greenwood.

Thompson, E. P. 1963. *The Making of the English Working Class.* London: Penguin.

Thompson, William R., and Richard M. Tucker. 1997. "A Tale of Two Democratic Peace Critiques." *Journal of Conflict Resolution* 41:428–54.

United Nations. 1950–96. *Yearbook of International Trade Statistics,* later renamed *International Trade Statistics Yearbook.* Annual. New York: Department of International Economic and Social Affairs Statistical Office.

U.S. Bureau of the Census. 1975. *Historical Statistics of the United States, Colonial Times to 1970.* Washington, DC: U.S. Department of Commerce.

U.S. Congress. 1917. *Trading with the Enemy Act of October 6, 1917.* In U.S.C.A.

Vasquez, John A. 1993. *The War Puzzle.* Cambridge Studies in International Relations, no. 27. Cambridge: Cambridge University Press.

———. 2000. *What Do We Know about War?* Lanham, MD: Rowman and Littlefield.

Viner, Jacob. 1937. *Studies in the Theory of International Trade.* New York and London: Harper and Brothers.

———. 1948. "Power versus Plenty as Objectives of Foreign Policy in the Seventeenth and Eighteenth Centuries." *World Politics* 1, no. 1: 1–29.

Vuchinich, Samuel, and Jay Teachman. 1993. "Influences on the Duration of Wars,

Strikes, Riots, and Family Arguments." *Journal of Peace Research* 37, no. 3: 544–68.

Wallensteen, Peter. 1973. *Structure and War: On International Relations 1920–1968.* Stockholm: Raben and Sjogren.

Waltz, Kenneth Neal. 1979. *Theory of International Politics.* Addison-Wesley Series in Political Science. Reading, MA: Addison-Wesley.

Walzer, Michael. 1976. *The Revolution of the Saints: A Study in the Origins of Radical Politics.* New York: Atheneum.

Ward, Michael D., and Kristian S. Gleditsch. 1998. "Democratizing for Peace." *American Political Science Review* 92, no. 1: 51–61.

Wattenberg, Ben J. 1976. *Introduction and User's Guide to the Statistical History of the United States from Colonial Times to the Present.* New York: Basic Books.

Wayman, Frank, and J. David Singer. 1990. "Evolution and Directions for Improvement in the Correlates of War Project Methodologies." In *Measuring the Correlates of War,* ed. J. David Singer and Paul F. Diehl. Ann Arbor: University of Michigan Press.

Weber, Max. 1958. *The Protestant Ethic and the Spirit of Capitalism.* Trans. Talcott Parsons. New York: Charles Scribner's Sons.

Weede, Erich. 1976. "Overwhelming Preponderance as a Pacifying Condition among Contiguous Asian Dyads." *Journal of Conflict Resolution* 20, no. 3: 395–411.

World Almanac Book of Facts. 1995. Mahwah, NJ: World Almanac Books.

World Bank. 1995. *World Data Series on CD-Rom* [CD-ROM]. World Bank.

World Bank International Economic Department. 1993. *World Tables of Economic and Social Indicators, 1950–1992 Codebook.* ICPSR 6159. Data supplied by the Inter-University Consortium for Political and Social Research.

Yates, P. Lamartine. 1959. *Forty Years of Foreign Trade: A Statistical Handbook with Special Reference to Primary Products and Under-Developed Countries.* London: Allen and Unwin.

Zavoina, R., and W. McElvey. 1975. "A Statistical Model for the Analysis of Ordinal Level Dependent Variables." *Journal of Mathematical Sociology* 4:103–20.

NAME INDEX

SUBJECT INDEX

Alliances, 12, 160n
  data, 160n
  and trade patterns, 34, 111, 112–18, 159–60nn. 22, 24
  variable, 65, 69, 73–74, 88, 90, 94, 101, 102
Asymmetrical dependence, 3, 28, 122, 123
  and conflict, 39–41, 69, 127, 130–33
  and hostility, 33
  and power, 28, 30, 31, 33, 65–66
  See also Dependence
Austria-Hungary, trade with major powers, 112–18, 149–56

Battle fatalities
  and interdependence, 90–93
  measure, 85

c.i.f., 141
Civil wars, 6–7, 80, 94, 108, 124
Class, economic, 19, 21, 35, 98
Close relationships, 6, 7, 32, 80–82, 94, 123, 136
Cold War, 1, 64, 117
  postwar era, 1, 48, 126, 128, 130
Colonialism, 127, 128, 140
Composite Index of National Capabilities (CINC), 66
Conflict, 108, 158n
  escalation of, 80, 84, 88–90, 93, 112
  evolution of, 79
  intensity of, 7, 80–82, 90, 92, 93
  measures of, 51
  resolution of, 80, 82, 87, 124, 125
  settlement of, 80, 82
  severity, 82, 85, 88, 90
  study of, 44

See also Militarized Interstate Dispute (MID)
Constructive engagement, 2, 32, 56
Contact, beliefs about, 6–7, 22, 26, 27, 35–37, 135–36
Contiguity, 62–63, 69, 87–88, 90, 101, 102, 135, 159n
Control variables, 4, 62–67, 69–70, 73, 74, 76, 84, 85, 87, 89–90, 100–102
  alliances, 65, 69, 73–74, 88, 90, 94, 101, 102
  contiguity, 62–63, 69, 87–88, 90, 101, 102, 135, 159n
  democracy, 63–65, 69–70, 87–88, 90, 91, 92, 93, 101, 102, 135–36, 159n
  peace-years measure, 66–67, 69
  power (capabilities), 65–66, 90, 101, 104
  temporal dependence, 66–67, 69
Cooperation, 21, 136, 158n
  coexistence with conflict, 7, 51, 81, 93, 95, 123, 125
  and interdependence, 2, 6
  and peace, 20, 50, 125
  and trade, 10
Correlates of War (COW) Project, 52, 66, 139, 143, 158n, 161n

Data
  alliance, 159n
  CINC, 66
  contiguity, 159nn. 17, 18
  exchange rates, 112, 143–44, 161n
  GDP, 72, 159n
  limitations of, 49–50, 55–56, 82, 100, 112, 160n
  Militarized Interstate Disputes, 52